Citizenship and the American Revolution

A Resolute Tory's Abiding Status

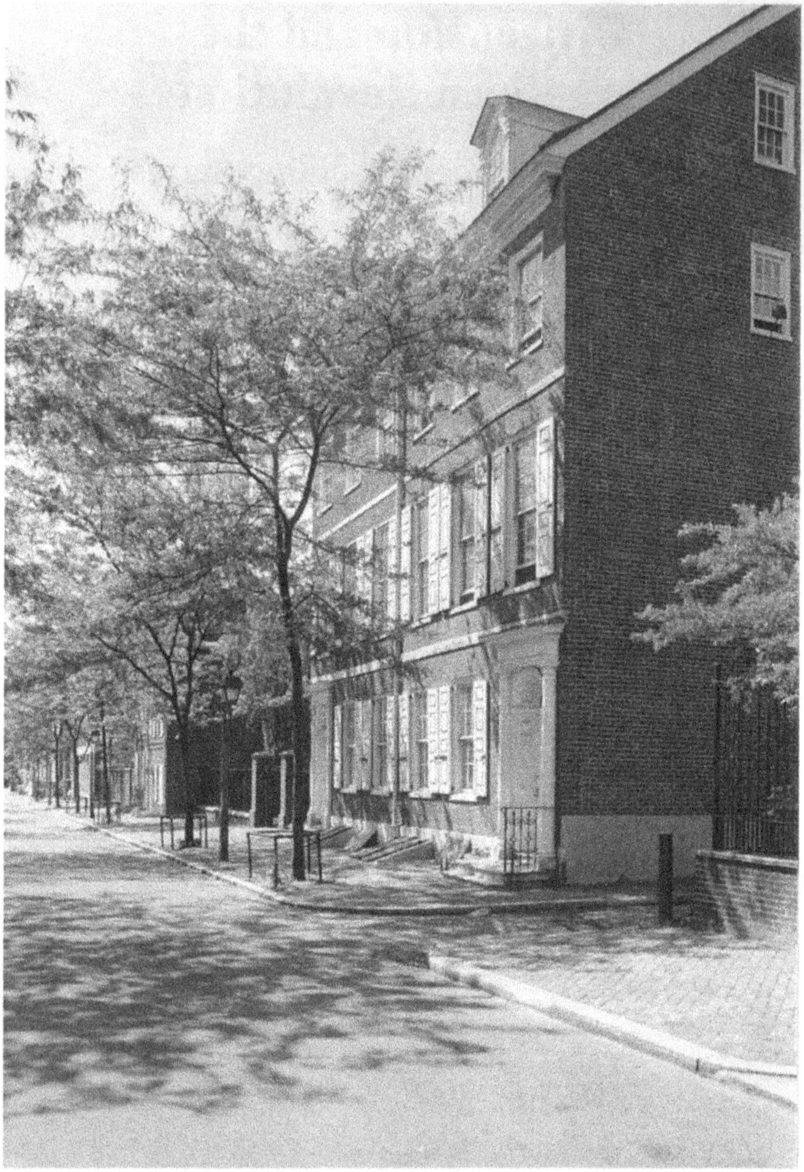

The Berry–Coxe house, as it appears today at 413 Locust Street, which Tench Coxe occupied as tenant during the pendency of the lawsuit (his address then being recorded as 11 Prune Street).

Courtesy of Library of Congress, HABS PA, 51-PHILA. 168-16

Citizenship and the American Revolution

A Resolute Tory's Abiding Status

David W. Maxey

American Philosophical Society Press
Philadelphia • 2016

Transactions of the
American Philosophical Society
Held at Philadelphia
For Promoting Useful Knowledge
Volume 106, Part 3

ISBN: 978-1-60618-063-1

U.S. ISSN: 0065-9746

Library of Congress Cataloging-in-Publication Data
Names: Maxey, David W. (David Walker), 1934- author.
Title: Citizenship and the American revolution : a resolute tory's abiding status / David W. Maxey.
Description: Philadelphia, PA : American Philosophical Society, 2016. | Includes index.
Identifiers: LCCN 2016036848 | ISBN 9781606180631 (alk. paper)
Subjects: LCSH: Citizenship—United States—History. | Citizenship, Loss of— United States—History. | Inheritance and succession—New Jersey—History. | Trials—New Jersey—History.
Classification: LCC KF4700 .M39 2016 | DDC 342.7308/3—dc23
LC record available at https://lccn.loc.gov/2016036848

For Cath–always

Contents

Preface

> He [Daniel Coxe] was on the 3d of July 1776, a subject of the king of Great-Britain; so was Hancock and Adams; so was General Washington and the band of patriots that composed his army, and must we gainsay their citizenship and declare them *aliens* to their country?
> —Gabriel H. Ford, of New Jersey Supreme Court (1829)[1]

How to account for this burst of judicial hyperbole more than a half century after the Declaration of Independence? Even at that late date, strange as it may seem, the basis on which a person acquired citizenship once independence was declared remained a matter for dispute. Did a previous subject of His Majesty the King immediately owe a duty of loyalty to the newly constituted government of the state in which he resided, or did he retain a right to confirm at some point his continuing allegiance to the king? If a dissenter became a citizen in spite of himself, could he nevertheless by subsequent action effectively cast aside that identity?

The justices of the Supreme Court of the United States did not find these questions easy to answer. Lacking any solid authority to lean on, they did their best to avoid answering them—until, in the twice-argued case of *McIlvaine v. Coxe's Lessee*,[2] they had no choice but to rule on the issue of citizenship acquired during the Revolution and its durability.

A steadfast adherent of the king's cause, Daniel Coxe left his native land in 1783 and entered into permanent exile in England. Almost immediately upon arriving there, he submitted a claim for substantial compensation to the commission Parliament had established to compensate loyalists for losses they had sustained during the Revolution. Later, twenty years after the Revolution had ended, he sought to participate in the intestate distribution of his aunt's valuable real estate, a result denied him under New Jersey law unless he could prove that in the intervening years he had remained a citizen of that state. It was his second

---

[1] *Coxe v. Gullick*, 10 N.J.L. (5 Halst.) 328, 330 (1829).
[2] 6 U.S. (2 Cranch) 280 (1805) and 8 U.S. (4 Cranch) 209 (1808).

claim—on the face of it, difficult to reconcile with the extensive evidence he had presented in support of the first one—that led to the Supreme Court's decision in *McIlvaine v. Coxe's Lessee.*

My objective in pursuing this inquiry has been to place in an informed historical perspective that proceeding and the parties, lawyers, and judges engaged in it. The Supreme Court's decision was not, moreover, the last word on citizenship acquired during the Revolution, and in the concluding pages of this study I explore the further evolution of judicial thinking on this subject.

I am again grateful to the American Philosophical Society for accepting a work of mine for publication.[3] As was true before, I have benefited from the critical review and comments of readers to whom the Society referred the manuscript. I am especially indebted to two distinguished legal historians, Barbara Aronstein Black and Stanley N. Katz, for their generous appraisal of what this amateur in their field produced. Finally, it has been a renewed pleasure to work with Mary McDonald, the Society's director of publications, who has patiently guided me along the path to publication.

David W. Maxey

---

[3] Thirty-two past members of the American Philosophical Society appear in either the text or the footnotes, although some of them became members after the Supreme Court's decision in 1808. The list is provided in the Appendix. For confirmation of APS membership, the Society's website has been consulted at http://www.amphilsoc.org/memhist/search.

List of Illustrations

Cover: The Capitol, Washington, DC, at the beginning of the nineteenth century, when the Supreme Court held its sessions in cramped committee room space in the new building. Watercolor by William Russell Birch, circa 1800. Workmen can be seen cutting stone in the left foreground.

Courtesy of Library of Congress, LC-USZC4-247

Frontispiece: The Berry–Coxe house, as it appears today at 413 Locust Street, which Tench Coxe occupied as tenant during the pendency of the lawsuit (his address then being recorded as 11 Prune Street).

Courtesy of Library of Congress, HABS PA, 51-PHILA, 168-16

1

The Death of a Wealthy Relation

— The Death of a Wealthy Relation —

On March 20, 1802, Rebecca Coxe died in her eighty-sixth year. She was buried in the family vault in St. Michael's Episcopal Church, across the street from her house in Trenton, New Jersey.

One of four children of Colonel Daniel and Sarah Eckley Coxe, she came into substantial property upon her father's death in 1739, consisting largely of real estate that he and his father before him had assembled. Never marrying and having limited needs, she kept intact the fortune she had inherited.[1] Practically nothing else is known about her. Family legend had it that she was engaged to a colonial governor of New Jersey, whom she "discharged," thereafter "retir[ing] from the world although beautiful and wealthy."[2]

However, one fact of critical importance is known about Rebecca Coxe: She died without a will. Why she failed to make a will is a matter for guesswork. Because of disabling infirmity, she may have lacked legal capacity to do so. Or she may have faltered in the task when confronted with the considerable property she owned in New Jersey and New York State and the complexity of apportioning it among her relatives. Or, like many others who have died without a will, she may have resisted acknowledging the encroaching end of her days.

Whatever the reason may have been, her failure to make a will fueled a family dispute over who was entitled to inherit the real estate she owned. Several of the country's foremost lawyers lined up as advocates in a lawsuit culminating in a decision that the U. S. Supreme Court reached in 1808, but not without apparent hesitancy. The contest that Rebecca Coxe's relatives pursued in court exposed fundamental questions that the Revolution left unresolved about the acquisition and possible loss of American citizenship.[3]

---

[1] For background information concerning the Coxe family and Rebecca Coxe's father, Colonel Daniel Coxe (*bapt.* 1673–1739), and her grandfather, Dr. Daniel Coxe (1640–1730), see G. D. Scull, "Biographical Notice of Dr. Daniel Coxe, of London," *Pennsylvania Magazine of History and Biography* (hereafter *PMHB*) 7 (1883): 317–37; Jacob E. Cooke's definitive biography, *Tench Coxe and the Early Republic* (Chapel Hill, NC: University of North Carolina Press, 1978), 3–13; and Frank William Leach and Alexander Du Bin, *Coxe Family* (Philadelphia: The Historical Publication Society, 1936). The extent of Colonel Daniel Coxe's vast landed estate, which he parceled out to his children (including three illegitimate children), may be measured in his will, the provisions of which are abstracted in *New Jersey Archives*, 1st ser. "Calendar of New Jersey Wills, Administrations, Etc., 1730–1750" (Somerville, NJ: The Unionist-Gazette Association, 1918), 21:118–20. Valuable information about the Coxe family appears in the extensive finding aid for the Coxe Family Papers, Collection No. 2049 (hereafter CFP), at the Historical Society of Pennsylvania (hereafter HSP), Philadelphia, PA. The finding aid is accessible online at: http://hsp.org/sites/default/files/legacy_files/migrated/findingaid2049coxe.pdf.

[2] Leach and Du Bin, *Coxe Family*, 14.

[3] The most comprehensive treatment of the evolving concept of American citizenship remains James H. Kettner's *The Development of American Citizenship, 1608–1870* (Chapel Hill, NC: University of North Carolina Press, 1978). Kettner is committed to the thesis that from the Revolution onward there was a steady progression toward "volitional citizenship"—whereby "the individual alone would be responsible for making the choice between subjectship and citizenship." Ibid., 208 (and chp. 7 generally). A more recent work is Douglas Bradburn's *The Citizenship Revolution: Politics and the Creation of the American Union, 1774–1804* (Charlottesville, VA: University of Virginia Press, 2009), which gives primary emphasis to the political divide between Federalists and Republicans and, ending as it does with Jefferson's first term, omits any reference to the arguments and decision in *McIlvaine v. Coxe's Lessee.*

2

Tory Cousins

T he controversy over Rebecca Coxe's estate pitted two branches of the Coxe family against each other. On one side were the children of her brother Daniel and his wife, Abigail Streate Coxe: a son Daniel and a daughter Grace.[1] On the other side were the children of her brother William and his wife, Mary Francis Coxe: John D., Tench, William, Jr., and Daniel W.[2] Of these first cousins, the principal antagonists were Daniel Coxe and Tench Coxe, each of them elected in his time a member of the American Philosophical Society—Daniel Coxe in 1772, and Tench Coxe in 1796. Not incidentally for present purposes, these two cousins shared the added distinction of being stubborn to the point of belligerence.

The Daniel Coxe who will henceforth be a focus of this study was born in Trenton in about 1741 and died in London in 1826. Before the Revolution, he practiced law in New Jersey and Pennsylvania, having been admitted to the New Jersey bar in 1761 and the Philadelphia bar four years later. Early in the Revolution, he allied himself with the British, leaving Trenton in late 1776 and eventually serving as a magistrate in British-occupied Philadelphia. When the British forces withdrew from Philadelphia in June 1778, Coxe accompanied the army to New York, where he repeatedly sought offices of consequence in the British administration while at the same time carrying on a covert correspondence with participants in the Benedict Arnold conspiracy. Upon the signing of the treaty of peace and the British departure from New York, he had no realistic choice but to leave for England, where he lived for the remainder of his life, never returning to the country of his birth.[3]

His sister Grace married John Tabor Kempe, a native of England who succeeded his father as attorney general of the colony of New York. The Kempes, too, were firmly attached to the British cause; they fled to England at the conclusion of the war, and their property in New York State was forfeited as penalty for their obduracy. As a widow, Grace Kempe would join her brother in the family litigation over their aunt's estate.[4]

Born into a wealthy and prominent Philadelphia family, Tench Coxe (Figure 1) was fourteen years younger than his cousin Daniel Coxe. Enrolled at age six

---

[1] Daniel Coxe, the father, was born in 1710 and died in late 1758 or early 1759. By royal appointment he was one of the principal burgesses of Trenton. Leach and Du Bin, *Coxe Family*, 14.

[2] William Coxe, the father, was born in 1723 and died in 1801. He was the first of the Coxe family to locate in Philadelphia, where he became one of the city's leading merchants and assumed a variety of public and private offices. He and his wife had thirteen children, not all of whom survived infancy; the four sons named in the text were involved in the family contest over their aunt's estate. Cooke, *Tench Coxe*, 11–13; and Leach and Du Bin, *Coxe Family*, 27–28.

[3] Edwin Robert Walker, et al., *A History of Trenton: 1679–1929* (Princeton, NJ: Princeton University Press, 1929), 141–42; Leach and Du Bin, *Coxe Family*, 15; and Ruma Chopra, *Unnatural Rebellion: Loyalists in New York City During the Revolution* (Charlottesville, VA: University of Virginia Press, 2011), 170–71. By one account Daniel Coxe was born in 1739. For Coxe's correspondence with the Arnold co-conspirators, see Carl Van Doren, *Secret History of the American Revolution* (New York: The Viking Press, 1941), 235–36, 411–13.

[4] Walker et al., *History of Trenton*, 142–43; Leach and Du Bin, *Coxe Family*, 15.

Figure 1. Portrait of Tench Coxe, by J. Paul, 1795, engraved by John Sartain.
Courtesy of the Historical Society of Pennsylvania.

as a student in the academy section of The College, Academy, and Charitable
School of Philadelphia, he did not progress far enough to obtain a degree from
the College of Philadelphia (later, the University of Pennsylvania). When he
came of age, he is said to have briefly considered a career in the law, following
in the footsteps of his older brother John, who went to England to prepare at the
Inns of Court; yet the easier alternative available to him, promising immediate
reward, was to enter his father's counting house as a junior partner in the firm
of Coxe Furman & Coxe, where he received an equal third share in the profits
of the enterprise.[5]

---

[5]Cooke, *Tench Coxe*, 11–18; one may chart his enrollment in the academy section of the College of
Philadelphia for a period of approximately ten years, beginning as early as 1761, in the tuition books of that
institution held in the University of Pennsylvania Archives and available online at: http://sceti.library.upenn.edu/
sceti/codex/public/pagelevel/index.cfm?workID=904

If Daniel Coxe openly proclaimed his allegiance to the crown, his younger cousin may have hesitated as he reflected on his father's advice to maintain a neutral position in the conflict. The firm's business prospered in the first months after the Declaration of Independence when scarcity in Philadelphia increased its profits. Even so, Tench Coxe realized by year's end that maintaining neutrality had itself become a hazardous occupation, incurring patriot wrath. The steady advance of the British army across New Jersey and the looming threat to Philadelphia persuaded him that the time had come to side with the British.[6]

After finding temporary refuge in New Jersey, he went to New York City, which was then and for the rest of the war in British hands and where Tory sympathizers warmly welcomed him. He remained in New York until General Howe mounted what seemed at first a leisurely summer campaign against the American army by landing major forces at the Head of the Elk on the eastern shore of the Chesapeake Bay. Coxe joined that expedition, not as a combatant but as an interested observer. Although his involvement cannot be traced exactly, he was probably present at the Battle of Brandywine, a British victory in September 1777. In partisan attacks launched against him in later years, Coxe is pictured as among those jovially accompanying General Cornwallis and his troops upon their triumphant entrance into Philadelphia at the end of that month.[7]

Tench Coxe stayed in Philadelphia for the duration of the British occupation of that city—from late September 1777 to the middle of June 1778. He took full advantage of the opportunities to make money in trading for his own benefit and for the British, sometimes crossing the line to engage in contraband transactions. Nor can there be any doubt that he had open access to both the British high command and the upper echelons of Philadelphia society consisting of those who felt at ease remaining in place when the city was under British control. By the marriages of his mother's siblings, he could claim as relatives members of the Willing, Tilghman, and Shippen families. In January 1778, he married Catherine McCall, the sister of Thomas Willing's wife, Anne. Their wedding, Coxe's biographer imagines, must have drawn "the cream of British officialdom, as well as many of Coxe's relatives and friends . . . making it one of the highlights of the city's social season." If so, Daniel Coxe, then installed as a magistrate appointed by General Sir William Howe, would surely have been among the guests.[8]

---

[6]Cooke, *Tench Coxe*, 16–21.

[7]Ibid., 21–26. The Coxe Papers at HSP contain a formal declaration by James Warren, a merchant of the City of London, confirming that he and Coxe were with the British marching northward from the Head of the Elk toward Philadelphia in August 1777 but stating that Coxe never engaged in or countenanced plundering. As the British were about to evacuate Philadelphia, Warren was apparently called on to assist Coxe in his defense against the charge that he had aided the British from an early date. James Warren, certification, June 12, 1778, CFP, box 8, folder 5.

[8]Cooke, *Tench Coxe*, 27–40. The speculation about the wedding as a grand social event is found at ibid., 34. Catherine Coxe, in poor health at the start of their marriage, died six months later. Four years after her death Coxe would take as his second wife Rebecca Coxe, his cousin and his grandfather's granddaughter through Colonel Daniel Coxe's liaison with a Mary Johnson of Trenton. Ibid., 10, 43, 54–55.

Under an attainder proclamation issued by the Pennsylvania Supreme Executive Council on May 21, 1778, these two Tory cousins found themselves identified in dangerous company. Among the several dozen people named in the proclamation, "who, it is said, have joined the Armies of the Enemy," were "Tench Coxe, Merchant," and "Daniel Coxe, heretofore of Trenton, in the State of New Jersey, Esq'r." The targeted individuals were directed to appear before a justice of the Supreme Court or a justice of the peace "on or before the Sixth day of July next ensuing, & also abide their legal tryal for such their Treasons, on pain that every of them not rendering himself as aforesaid, and abiding the tryal aforesaid, shall from and after the Sixth day of July next, stand & be attainted of High Treason."[9]

Faced with this stern message and on notice that the British were about to abandon Philadelphia and their allies there, Tench Coxe nevertheless decided to stay in the city and gamble on the leniency of the returning patriots. His wife's declining health unquestionably contributed to that decision. He joined others in Philadelphia whose position had been at least equivocal about independence by taking the prescribed oath of allegiance to the Commonwealth of Pennsylvania while foreswearing any and all attachment to the crown. To comply with the statutory requirement, these Whig converts needed to seek out a magistrate duly empowered to certify their compliance, which Coxe succeeded in doing on May 23, 1778. For his cousin Daniel Coxe, so prominently in the employ of the British, such a high-risk bet was inconceivable; he accompanied the departing British to New York, leaving his wife and children in Philadelphia to fend for themselves.[10]

Despite his having openly engaged in trade with the enemy, Tench Coxe avoided standing trial for treason. Youth may have counted in his favor, but the more telling factor that operated to save him was his father and his father's well-placed friends, especially Thomas McKean, then Chief Justice of Pennsylvania, who presided over a succession of treason trials in Philadelphia that began in the fall of 1778. Coxe had a reassuring interview with McKean in July; his case never came to trial, and by official dispensation the dark cloud of attainder that had hung ominously over his head lifted.[11]

What chastening effect did this experience have on Tench Coxe? Very little that one can discern, for the charge of duplicity would follow him the rest of his

---

[9]Minutes of Supreme Executive Council, May 21, 1778, *Colonial Records of Pennsylvania*, 16 vols. (Harrisburg, PA: 1838–1853), 11:493–95. The Council voted on this proclamation in Lancaster, to which the Pennsylvania authorities had retreated during the British occupation of Philadelphia.

[10]Cooke, *Tench Coxe*, 37–42. The oath of allegiance Coxe took as certified by John Knowles is found in CFP, box 8, folder 3. Daniel Coxe married Sarah Redman in 1771; his wife's father, an eminent physician, was the preceptor of Benjamin Rush, who in turn would take as his pupil another distinguished physician, John Redman Coxe (1773–1864), the son of Daniel and Sarah Redman Coxe. *The Autobiography of Benjamin Rush; His "Travels Through Life" together with his Commonplace Book for 1789–1813*, ed. George W. Corner (Princeton, NJ: Princeton University Press, 1948), 37–39, 74n90.

[11]See Cooke, *Tench Coxe*, 42–43, for his father's influence and the interview with McKean. For the discharge by proclamation, see *Pennsylvania Packet*, Dec. 12, 1778.

life. Although he became an ardent supporter of the national government, an office holder in it, and a prolific promoter and pamphleteer, he remained temperamentally headstrong and a gambler at heart, inclined to shift allegiances as he perceived it opportune to do so.[12]

---

[12] On Tench Coxe's reputation, see Cooke, *Tench Coxe*, 44–45, 126–28, 309–10, 340–41, 380–81. Coxe's major work as an author was *A View of the United States of America, in a Series of Papers Written Between the Years 1787 and 1794* (Philadelphia: William Hall and Wrigley & Berriman, 1794). Even before he had hit full stride as pamphleteer and author, his fellow Pennsylvanian Senator William Maclay recorded in his journal that "[Coxe] was deeply affected with the literary itch, *cacoethes scribendi*." *The Journal of William Maclay: United States Senator from Pennsylvania, 1789–1791*, ed. Edgar S. Maclay (New York: D. Appleton and Company, 1890), 258 (May 7, 1790).

3

Daniel Coxe, Loyalist Claimant

Daniel Coxe paid a heavy price for his loyalty to the king. In severing so decisively every connection with his native land, he lost substantial property and the assurance of a comfortable life for his wife, his children, and himself. As soon as he arrived in London, he began working on a claim for compensation to submit to the commission appointed by Parliament in 1783 "to enquire into the losses and services of all such persons who have suffered in their rights, properties, and professions during the late unhappy dissensions in America in consequence of their loyalty to his Majesty and attachment to the British Government."[1]

In pursuing his claim as a lawyer acting for himself, he proved an untiring advocate, although sometimes not knowing when to stop and at least on one occasion incurring the displeasure of the commissioners for overreaching. In early January 1784, he applied for interim relief, asking the commissioners to restore the allowance "which he received from Government in America," but which had ceased with the evacuation of New York. To this first communication he appended notice of what he estimated to be the magnitude of the overall losses he had sustained: "As near as Mr. Coxe can at present form an idea of his losses in America, his Papers being as yet wholly deranged, he believes they must amount to near if not upwards of Thirty Thousand pounds sterling."[2]

Two months later Coxe submitted a full-blown memorial to the commissioners. The first nine manuscript pages were a narrative recital of Coxe's status and possessions "previous to the late Troubles in America" and of his "invariable opposition to the late seditious Usurpations in America," which exposed him to "much personal Insult and Danger, insomuch that on the advance of the British Army into the Jersies in December 1776, he was obliged hastily to withdraw himself and his Family into Pennsylvania." He abandoned his house in Trenton, "with all the Furniture standing intire [sic] and every other Domestic Article complete, under the Care of his Servants, as was usual for him to do when he removed his Family to Philadelphia for the Winter Season, intending to embrace the first favorable opportunity of returning."

---

[1] For background on the Loyalist Claims Commission, see Wallace Brown, *The King's Friends: The Composition and Motives of the American Loyalist Claimants* (Providence, RI: Brown University Press, 1965), 127–53, 257, 317–21; Mary Beth Norton, *The British-Americans: The Loyalist Exiles in England, 1774–1789* (Boston: Little, Brown, 1972), 185–222; and Maya Jasanoff, *Liberty's Exiles: American Loyalists in the Revolutionary World* (New York: Alfred A. Knopf, 2011), 113–45.

[2] The records of the Loyalist Claims Commission have been preserved in the National Archives of Great Britain at Kew. These Audit Office (AO) records are available on microfilm at various repositories in the United States, including the David Library at Washington Crossing, PA, identified either as AO 12 (film 263) or AO 13 (film 264), followed by volume and page or folio number. Coxe's initial memorial of Jan. 5, 1784, is found at AO 13/108/358-62. He was awarded an annual allowance of £200 to be increased to £300 once his family arrived in England, which occurred on July 30, 1785. See Coxe's application for additional support and the decision of the Loyalist Claims Commission, Aug. 1785, AO 12/101/236–37. The present purchasing power in pounds sterling of the increased allowance of 1785 comes to £34,200 (http://www.measuringworth.com/).

To return proved impossible because, "Trenton and its vicinities becoming now most unfortunately the principal Scene of War," his house and estate were commandeered as headquarters for the Hessian troops, "and notwithstanding his well known public and loyal Character & every remonstrance of his friends & Servants . . . his Rooms, Closets, Stores & Cellars were all broke open ransacked and pillaged, & every species of Furniture, China, Glass Liquors &c plundered destroyed or taken away." Confronted with reports of this devastation rendering his property in Trenton "utterly untenantable," he was compelled with his family "to live for several Months near Philadelphia in the most anxious Dread and Obscurity, until the British took possession of that city in Sept 1777."[3]

Coxe outlined the various services he had performed for the British army, starting with the commission he received in Philadelphia from General Howe to act as a magistrate of police at an annual compensation of £300 sterling. He took credit for having used his influence to raise among the Jersey loyalists a corps of men and officers called the "West Jersey Volunteers" who assisted in the foraging effort for supplies and "in other material services." Coxe was commended by General Howe for this recruitment effort, which Coxe cited as "perhaps the only Instance in America during the War in which a private Gentleman's Influence was directed in this way without an Expence of Bounty in the first instance to the Crown or of any Emolument whatever to himself."[4] When the British evacuated Philadelphia in June 1778, and at the cost of "every private and domestic Feeling, he was forced to abandon his Family and Property, and retire with the Army to New York for protection." Thereafter and "in consequence of his Service Zeal and Attachment to the Royal Cause, he became attainted in Pennsylvania and proscribed in Jersey," all of his property in the latter province being confiscated "by the usurped powers." His wife and four children were thrown on the charity of family and friends and stayed in Philadelphia until they were expelled in the summer of 1780 by the Executive Council of Pennsylvania, when they joined Coxe in New York. Rather than become a "useless burthen to Government here [in England]," Coxe remained in New York, "looking forward to the probable moment when his deluded Countrymen would perceive the Madness of their Conduct, and the Folly of their Independent Views, or [when] the Operations of the British Arms w[oul]d again reunite the Colonies to the British Empire."

During his stay in New York, "he carried on Private Correspondence out of the Lines and at his own Expence procured and furnished to the then Commander in Chief a variety of useful Intelligence." He received an "unsolicited appointment" as a member of the Board of Directors of the Associated Loyalists within the British lines; in June 1781, he was appointed assistant secretary to His

---

[3] Memorial of Daniel Coxe, March 13, 1784, AO 12/13/181–82.
[4] Ibid., AO 12/13/183.

Majesty's Commissioners for restoring Peace to the Colonies, and later became a member of that body, remaining in that position, at a salary of twenty shillings a day, until the British evacuation of New York; in April 1783, at the request of Sir Guy Carleton, he also agreed to serve as a member of the board Carleton established to settle and adjust matters of debt and to assume "several other Confidential Trusts connected with the same Board."[5]

Affecting a deferential approach, Coxe laid out his claim for compensation before the commissioners. For someone who had pleaded two months before that his papers were "wholly deranged," he succeeded in setting forth a detailed schedule and valuation of his losses of income and real and personal property, as annexed to the memorial and running another ten manuscript pages. The bottom line in his particularized submission was a claim for compensation totaling £40,267.11.6 sterling.[6]

The commission held evidentiary hearings on Coxe's claim over five days at the end of November and the beginning of December 1784. Coxe was the first to testify, followed by a number of witnesses, including Joseph Galloway, to whom Coxe, as magistrate, reported in Philadelphia; Governor William Franklin, the last Royal Governor of New Jersey, and Benjamin Franklin's outspoken loyalist son; and Samuel Shoemaker, a Quaker and former Philadelphia mayor, who for his loyalist sympathies fled Philadelphia and later New York. The dozen witnesses who appeared to testify on behalf of Coxe supported his claim, but not in every respect, and sometimes the testimony they gave was sufficiently qualified or tepid that it undercut his case. For example, Samuel Shoemaker, after affirming that Coxe's character was "uniformly that of a Loyalist," remarked that Coxe's large property holdings were "not very productive" and that his estate "consisted very much of uncultivated Lands," subject to wide swings in value.[7]

Daniel Coxe felt seriously aggrieved by the commission's decision respecting his claim. The commissioners reduced the award to £9,997, applying a 75% discount to Coxe's claim for compensation. What pained him particularly was the paltry advance payment he received of £3,298.4.0, of which he complained at length in an injudicious letter addressed to the secretary to the commission, John Forster, requesting a further hearing on deficiencies that the commissioners may have perceived in the proofs of loss he had provided. Although Forster's reply is missing, it's easy enough to measure its impact on Coxe, who tried to

---

[5] Ibid., AO 12/13/183–85. For Coxe's "Private Correspondence out of the Lines," see Van Doren, *Secret History*, 411-13.

[6] Ibid., AO 12/13/185–89 for the balance of the memorial; the annexed schedule and valuation appear at AO 12/13/189–99, with the total figure struck at AO 12/13/199. Based on http://www.measuringworth.com/, the present purchasing power of Daniel Coxe's 1784 claim would come to £4,430,000.

[7] Evidence on the foregoing memorial of Daniel Coxe, with a beginning date of Nov. 29, 1784, appears at AO 12/13/202–52. Shoemaker's testimony is at AO 12/13/249–50. Another character witness, Bernard La Grange, who, like Coxe, practiced law in New Jersey, testified that "he was not one of the most eminent [in the profession]." AO 12/13/234–35.

atone for his indiscretion by backtracking in apologetic tones: "I have the honor of your obliging answer to my Letter of the 27th ult, conveying the Commissioners Negative to my Requests ~ had I conceived these to have been of the nature you state them, I certainly should not have allowed myself to give the Trouble I have done."[8]

Did Coxe's claim appear inflated in the eyes of the commissioners? No doubt it did, although they were accustomed to applicants routinely overstating their losses. When the commission issued its final report in 1790, approximately £3 million had been awarded on aggregate claims of something over £10 million, so that in percentage terms, the discount applied to Coxe's claim was not that far off the average.[9]

At one particular claim of Coxe's, the commissioners may well have looked askance. Toward the end of his memorial he dwelt on a loss "which tho' not, perhaps, an object of clear present charge," he saw "materially affecting his future expectations." As a presumptive heir of "an antient Maiden Relation in America," he took for granted that on her death he would inherit valuable landed property "which she possesses in the Provinces of Jersey and York," as well as her personal property in bonds and other securities, of an aggregate value of upwards of £10,000 sterling. Yet punitive legislation passed in New Jersey against those adhering to the king would deprive him of this inheritance.[10]

In a subsequent letter to Forster, he dismissed any thought that his aunt might execute a will leaving her estate to others: "She is near 70, and incapable of making a Will from her present Infirmities, so that this Law, made during and as a consequence of the late Rebellion, affects him as deeply as he had the honor to state to the Commissioners in his Hearing, and agreeably to the list of her estate then delivered." Coxe regarded "the loss of near £10,000 Sterling" from Rebecca Coxe's estate as certain to him "as if the contingencies of her Death, and dying without a Will, had already happened."[11]

It is unlikely that the commissioners accepted any part of this submission, which took as a present loss attributable to his loyalist status the inheritance

---

[8]The amounts allowed Coxe on his claim may be found in "Proceedings of the said Commissioners of American Claims . . . containing The Reports and Statements of the said Commissioners, The Names of the Claimants, The Amount of their Claims & The Liquidation thereof," at AO 12/109/108. For Coxe's injudicious letter and his apology, see Coxe to Forster, Feb. 27 and March 10, 1786, AO 13/93/277–78, 287.

[9]The final figures are reported in Norton, *The British-Americans*, 185–222; and Jasanoff, *Liberty's Exiles*, 113–45.

[10]Memorial of Daniel Coxe, March 13, 1784, AO 12/13/187. In pressing his claim for compensation, Coxe took the position that under the law of New Jersey he was excluded from inheriting any part of his aunt's estate. Twenty years later, in litigation we are about to consider, his counsel would contend the opposite.

[11]Coxe to John Forster, Aug. 18, 1785, AO 13/93/270–71.

that Coxe might have realized had he survived his aunt. In point of fact, surviving Rebecca Coxe required a much longer wait than he could have foreseen. This "antient Maiden Relation," defying the calculations of her expectant relatives, lived for another eighteen years, before expiring at last in 1802.

4

The Question of Alienage

Having long anticipated the death of their wealthy relative, members of the Coxe family lost little time in projecting their distributable shares in Rebecca Coxe's estate. She died on a Saturday, and on Monday following, Daniel Coxe's father-in-law, Dr. John Redman, his son, Dr. John Redman Coxe, and the British consul in Philadelphia, Phineas Bond, filed of public record a caveat "against any paper purporting to be last will and testament of said Rebecca Coxe, or against granting any letters of administration until we shall have been first heard." Letters of administration were, however, granted three days later on March 25, 1802, to William Coxe, of the City of Burlington, Tench Coxe's younger brother.[1]

For Tench Coxe, his aunt's death and the money he expected to receive from her estate appeared a welcome gift from providence. He had incurred both mounting debts and his elderly father's increasing impatience and displeasure with his son's profligate ways. In 1800, Tench Coxe made a general assignment of his property to trustees in an attempt to safeguard his lands against the claims of creditors. William Coxe, Sr., Tench's father, died in October 1801, six months before his sister; he provided in his will for outright distribution to his children other than Tench Coxe, whose share he placed in trust.[2] Given his straitened condition, one may appreciate the letter Tench Coxe received shortly after his aunt's death from his good friend and lawyer, Peter Stephen Du Ponceau (Figure 2): "I congratulate you," wrote Du Ponceau, "on your late accession of fortune, & more so in the use which you intend to make of it, which I hope will prove as advantageous to you as it is honorable."[3]

How much an "accession of fortune" this might amount to depended on the resolution of a legal issue concerning Daniel Coxe's status under New Jersey law, which governed the distribution of Rebecca Coxe's estate. During the course of the last twenty years in England, and indeed previously while in this country, Daniel Coxe had identified himself time and again as a loyal British subject. Had he, therefore, completely shed his American identity, making him under New Jersey law an "alien"?

The common law held that a person not born within the dominions of the king of England was an alien and, with limited exceptions, prohibited from acquiring title to real estate by purchase or inheritance. In contrast, that prohibition did

---

[1] *New Jersey Archives*, 1st ser. "Calendar of New Jersey Wills, Administrations, Etc., 1801–1805" (Trenton, NJ: MacCrellish & Quigley Co., 1946), 39:106–07. William Coxe, Jr. (1762–1831), was a vestryman of St. Mary's Church in Burlington, a speaker of the New Jersey Assembly, and a member of the U.S. Congress from 1813 to 1815. He was also a recognized authority on the cultivation of fruit trees. Leach and Du Bin, *Coxe Family*, 47.

[2] Cooke, *Tench Coxe*, 337–38, 410–12.

[3] Du Ponceau to Coxe, Mar. 26, 1802, CFP, box 63, folder 10. Coxe docketed the letter "honorable notice of my use of Aunt Ra's late property."

Figure 2. Portrait of Peter S. Du Ponceau, by Thomas Sully, circa 1835, when Du Ponceau was president of the American Philosophical Society.

Courtesy of the American Philosophical Society.

not prevent aliens from inheriting personal property—furniture, jewelry, bonds, cash, and the like.[4]

Following the Revolution, many of the former colonies adopted these common-law rules and applied them to the distribution of the estates of those dying without

---

[4]W. S. Holdsworth, *A History of English Law*, 16 vols. (London: Methuen & Co., 1903–1966), 9:72–104 ("Subjects and Aliens"); Frederick Pollock and Frederick William Maitland, *The History of English Law Before the Time of Edward I*, 2 vols. (Boston: Little, Brown, 1899), 1:458–67 ("Aliens"). The different treatment of real and personal property in the law of intestate succession may be explained by the fact that the common-law courts regulated the former and ecclesiastical courts, the latter. See Lawrence R. Friedman, *A History of American Law*, 3rd ed. (New York: Simon & Schuster, 2005), 29–30; Sir Henry Sumner Maine, *Ancient Law: Its Connection With the Early History of Society and Its Relation to Modern Ideas*, 10th ed. (London: John Murray, 1885), 173.

a will. New Jersey was one such jurisdiction doing so. If, as a matter of law, Daniel Coxe was classified an alien, he would have been excluded from taking any part of his late aunt's landed estate, all of which would have then belonged to Tench Coxe and his siblings. To determine Daniel Coxe's status, however, required dealing with the American Revolution's disruptive influence on established relations and on the concept of allegiance.

Over the years of his residence abroad, Daniel Coxe had developed a close relationship with Margaret Shippen Arnorld, Benedict Arnold's wife and the daughter of Edward Shippen, Jr., of Philadelphia. Coxe had performed any number of services for Peggy Arnold, for which she expressed her gratitude in letters to her father. Shortly after Rebecca Coxe's death, Edward Shippen, then Chief Justice of Pennsylvania, wrote his daughter in London: "I feel very grateful to Mr. Coxe for his very kind exertions in your behalf: if it should ever be in my power to show my sense of them, I shall immediately demonstrate it more than by words. I am glad to find by the death of his Aunt Rebecca Coxe that he will probably come in for a part of her Estate which I am told in land & money will amount to the value of near two Hundred thousand Dollars."[5]

In May 1802, Shippen wrote directly to Daniel Coxe offering his help even though he understood that Phineas Bond, the British consul, had already advised Coxe on his legal position. Shippen recognized that "the only point that can possibly affect the case to your disadvantage" was "the question of alienage" which "has been taken up in different lights in different States."

Presumably possessed of inside knowledge that the Tench Coxe side had not yet obtained the opinion of counsel on this subject, he recommended that Daniel Coxe "take the Opinion of good Counsel in the State of New York" where valuable real estate interests were at stake. Shippen proposed the names of Alexander Hamilton and Brockholst Livingston, saying that he intended to pass that suggestion along to Daniel Coxe's son John. It seemed something of a pious afterthought for the Chief Justice to conclude: "The family here would no doubt take all they have a legal right to, but I believe do not wish to act an unfriendly, much less an unfair part by you or your Sister."[6]

---

[5] Shippen to Margaret Arnold Mar. 28, 1802, in Lewis Burd Walker, "Life of Margaret Shippen, Wife of Benedict Arnold," *PMHB* 26 (1902): 322–23. In a series of *PMHB* issues beginning in 1900, Walker published a biographical essay and a collection of Shippen family letters. Margaret Arnold died in 1804, and Daniel Coxe was one of the executors named under her will. Based on Chief Justice Shippen's estimate, the present purchasing power of $200,000 in 1802 would come to $4,560,000 (http://www.measuringworth.com/).

[6] Shippen to Daniel Coxe, May 13, 1802, in Walker, "Life of Margaret Shippen," *PMHB* 26 (1902): 328–29. In fact, Daniel Coxe had written Alexander Hamilton in 1787, inquiring about his landed property in the State of New York and asking for Hamilton's advice on "whether or not, and how far, the Principle of *Alienism*, is adopted seriously by your State, or Law Courts, or intended to be put into Execution on any event occurring on the Death of any Landholder, being a *British Subject*." There is no evidence that Hamilton ever replied. Coxe to Hamilton, London, Apr. 4, 1787, in *The Papers of Alexander Hamilton*, ed. Harold C. Syrett (New York: Columbia University Press, 1962), 4:141.

Both sides began the search for authoritative answers. The Coxe brothers opposed to Daniel Coxe approached counsel in New Jersey and New York to obtain their opinions on the disability of alienage as barring his claim to their aunt's estate, but with not uniform results. William Griffith, a respected member of the New Jersey Bar and one of John Adams's "Midnight Judges,"[7] prefaced his opinion with the statement that "This question involves consequences of laws on which it is probably a Difference of professional sentiments may be expected and ably supported." Griffith nevertheless went on to express "a sincere and decided opinion that Daniel Coxe and Grace Kempe are aliens." As to personal property, they were entitled to share in the distribution, but regarding the real estate in New Jersey they were barred from taking lands by descent—with the share that they would have taken but for their alien status devolving upon the other heirs who may lawfully inherit.[8]

Tench Coxe sought the opinion of two distinguished New York lawyers concerning Daniel Coxe's ability to take by inheritance real estate in New York, only to learn that Egbert Benson and Edward Livingston were of the view that Daniel Coxe and his sister were not barred from taking property in New York. When forwarding this unwelcome opinion, Edward Livingston tried to make partial amends to Tench Coxe: "We have recd the liberal fee directed to be paid for this Opinion which I hope may be expounded with sufficient precision to be clearly understood and to meet the Doubts on the Case; should any information however be deemed necessary we shall hold ourselves ready to give it without any additional charge."[9]

Tench Coxe registered surprise and disappointment upon receipt of the Livingston–Benson opinion. Egbert Benson, another "Midnight Judge" and a retired member of New York's highest court, wrote soothingly to Coxe: "You may be assured we meant to be as full and explicit as we supposed you expected. You estimate that opinions opposite to ours have been given by other Counsel. It is possible that we may be in error, and if so the sooner we may discover it the better." But Benson had one final nail to bang into the coffin by referring to an opinion of "our Supreme Court, in Oct. Term 1800, on the subject of the alienism of the <u>antenati</u>, or rather more precisely their Capacity to acquire, either by descent or Purchase, and to hold Lands." He offered to send the opinion, "if it

---

[7] Federalist judges appointed by Adams in the waning days of his administration to circuit courts created under the short-lived Judiciary Act of 1801.

[8] Opinion of William Griffith, Esq., Burlington, June 7, 1802, CFP, box 64, folder 3. Griffith, who had an ongoing role in the early stages of the litigation concerning Rebecca Coxe's estate, later abandoned his law practice, for which he was eminently qualified, to engage in business speculations, for which he decidedly wasn't. Elias Boudinot, his wife's uncle, bailed him out of trouble. George Adams Boyd, *Elias Boudinot: Patriot and Statesman, 1740–1821* (Princeton, NJ: Princeton University Press, 1952), 287–88. For Griffith's selection as a "Midnight Judge," see Kathryn Turner, "The Midnight Judges," *University of Pennsylvania Law Review* 109 (1961): 511–12.

[9] Livingston to Coxe, Aug. 31, 1802, CFP, box 64, folder 8.

has not gone astray," to Tench Coxe, "from which you will perceive that the Law, as it respects the Case of Mr. D. C. and Mrs. K, their capacity to take by Descent . . . is perhaps to be considered as <u>adjudged</u>, and consequently settled."[10]

In submitting the Livingston–Benson opinion to his brothers, and soliciting their views on the step next to take, Tench Coxe wrote that he wished the issue "were fairly, calmly and regularly before the Supreme Court of the United States. I confess I cannot doubt the law to be fully with us in the case."[11] Prior to Coxe's obtaining the opinion from New York counsel, Dr. John Redman Coxe had pressed him for the opportunity to review "the papers relative to the question of alienage of which you some time since furnished me with an abstract. As this is a question in which both families are interested, it is certainly desirable on what ground we mutually stand."[12] Both sides realized that a court proceeding was inevitable, but what might be the proper approach to take in obtaining a definitive ruling from the U.S. Supreme Court absorbed the attention and ingenuity of lawyers representing both branches of the family.

Article III of the U.S. Constitution included as within the judicial power of the United States controversies "between Citizens of different States" and "between a State, or the Citizens thereof, and foreign States, Citizens or Subjects." Assuming that the controversy could be framed in agreed-upon terms, there were two possible routes to a trial determination in federal court and an appeal taken thereafter to the Supreme Court. In exercise of the classic diversity jurisdiction, the suit might be structured as one between citizens of different states, or alternatively as one between a citizen or subject of a foreign state and a citizen or citizens of one of the United States.

The lawyers advising Daniel Coxe and his sister were of divided minds on how to proceed. Richard Stockton, of Princeton, the son of the signer of the Declaration of the same name, provided this advice in a letter to Phineas Bond:

> In what Court shall the suits be brought? Would it not be best for your friends to convey to some Citizen of Penna their estates on any trust they see fit and to institute the suits in the Circuit Court of the U.S.? If we are to succeed in our Supreme Court what should we do before the Court of Errors [New Jersey's highest court] composed of a majority of violent ignorant men, knowing nothing of law and acting from resentment and party feeling—and Tench Coxe our adversary. Our situation in this respect is indeed melancholy—but it is not to be conceded—you know eno[ugh] of it. This conveyance might even yet be executed and sent over before the next Circuit Court which is in April.

---

[10] Benson to Coxe, Dec. 7, 1802, CFP, box 65, folder 4. For Benson's appointment as a "Midnight Judge," see Turner, "The Midnight Judges," 503–04. The case Benson referred to was *Kelly v. Harrison*, 2 Johns. Cas. 29 (NY Sup. Ct., 1800), a decision in which Benson had participated as a member of the court.

[11] Coxe to Brothers, Sept. 8, 1802 (retained copy), CFP, box 64, folder 9.

[12] John Redman Coxe to Coxe, July 24, 1802, CFP, box 64, folder 6.

Stockton put his finger on the difficulty of following the alternative route of bringing suit on behalf of Daniel Coxe as an alien: "It would seem rather awkward to go into Court as Aliens [for jurisdictional purposes] and be obliged to contend in that Court that we are not Aliens [and therefore capable of inheriting]."[13]

Yet there was a real problem in seeking to achieve diversity jurisdiction by Daniel Coxe's conveying his interest in Rebecca Coxe's Trenton real estate, as Stockton recommended, to a nominal Pennsylvania trustee, whereupon an action in ejectment would be brought against an obscure member of the Coxe family, who resided in New Jersey.[14] Edward Tilghman, another lawyer advising Daniel Coxe, was adamant that this clever stratagem would not survive judicial scrutiny: "If under the Laws of Jersey, it would be fatal to Mr. Coxe's claim for him to cloath himself in the Garb of an alien or foreign Citizen in Suit, I much fear that no Conveyance to a Third Person, merely for the Purpose of giving jurisdiction to the federal Courts, would answer that Purpose."[15]

Tilghman had cogent support for his analysis in the case of *Maxfield's Lessee v. Levy* (1797), in which Justice Iredell of the Supreme Court, sitting on circuit, expressed outrage that his court should have been imposed upon by an unscrupulous party who, as a citizen of Pennsylvania, had brought suit "under the name of a citizen of another state, to whom it is alleged, conveyances were made without any consideration, for the sole purpose of making him a nominal lessor of the plaintiff in these ejectments." In attempted extenuation, counsel for the plaintiff pleaded that the creation of the trust was a mere harmless fiction to which the law had frequent recourse. Iredell would have none of that argument:

> It is sufficient to say of all of these [fictions], that they originally took place, when very dark notions of law and liberty were entertained; that they are supported now solely on the authority of long usage; and that no court would dare to set up a new one: No court in America ever yet thought, nor, I hope, ever will, of acquiring jurisdiction by a fiction. And the only fiction ever in general use in America ... I believe, has been that of proceeding by ejectment, which is a mere form of action, and so modified as to do no possible injury.[16]

[13] Stockton to Bond, Dec. 28, 1802, Jan. 13, 1803, Cadwalader Family Papers, Collection 1454 at HSP (hereafter CadP), box 206, folders 7 and 8. The Cadwalader Family Papers is another extensive collection of material at HSP that provides informed access to Daniel Coxe and his counsel. Phineas Bond's papers found their way into this collection because he was the brother-in-law of General John Cadwalader.

[14] Tench Coxe's sister Rebecca married William McIlvaine, a physician, and they had one daughter, Rebecca McIlvaine, born in 1783 just as her mother died. As the litigation began to take shape, this niece of Tench Coxe's possessed the convenient advantage of being a resident of New Jersey. Leach and Du Bin, *Coxe Family*, 46.

[15] Tilghman to Bond, Jan. 27, 1803, CadP, box 206, folder 8.

[16] *Maxfield's Lessee v. Levy*, 4 U.S. (4 Dall.) 331, 334 (Cir. Ct., PA Dist. 1797). The culprit in this case was the notorious land speculator Samuel Wallis, who had as a partner in his speculative activity Iredell's colleague on the bench, Justice James Wilson. See Charles Page Smith, *James Wilson: Founding Father, 1742–1798* (Chapel Hill, NC: University of North Carolina Press, 1956), 361, 366–67, 389–90.

Little wonder that, on the strength of this ruling, Edward Tilghman was convinced that the proposed attempt to manufacture diversity was ill-advised. He adhered to that view in a follow-up letter: "Since my letter to you, not a doubt has occurred to me as to the Impropriety of a Conveyance to give Jurisdiction."[17]

The benefit of contrived diversity was deemed, however, to outweigh the risks. Stockton and Griffith were instructed by their clients to work out the terms of submission to the U.S. Circuit Court for the District of New Jersey. Slowly a narrative emerged on which the two parties could agree. In the Cadwalader Family Papers at the Historical Society of Pennsylvania is an undated draft of a document, docketed "DC v. TC &tc," which sets forth the essential elements of the case, but with blanks left to be filled in and objections noted in the margin. Dr. John Redman Coxe sent a letter to Tench Coxe that appears to be the source of these objections, relating more to form than to substance, and that he ends by expressing "regret about the delay which has occurred but hope nothing further will intervene to prevent the Case being brought to issue as soon as possible."[18] In that sentiment, Tench Coxe emphatically concurred, instructing his Philadelphia lawyers, William Tilghman and Peter Du Ponceau, to take every measure necessary to initiate the litigation in the Circuit Court in New Jersey and thereafter to take an appeal to the Supreme Court of the United States.[19]

The relatively straightforward narrative the parties finally agreed on had to be recast, so Griffith advised his client, in the form of a special verdict, "a State of the Case not being sufficient to ground a Writ of Error on."[20] What came of all of this effort was a highly stylized document, a special verdict, which the Circuit Court, consisting of Justice Bushrod Washington and District Judge Robert Morris, acted on in early April. As the procedural means for determining title to real estate, the parties utilized the action in ejectment that Justice Iredell had labeled in *Maxfield's Lessee v. Levy* "the only fiction ever in general use in America . . . a mere form of action, and so modified as to do no possible injury."[21]

Although Justice Iredell may have underestimated the legal profession's reliance on other fictions, it is true that the action in ejectment, for all of its fictitious character, had come to serve a useful purpose in allowing the law to dispose of

[17]Tilghman to Bond, Feb. 1, 1803, CadP, box 206, folder 8.

[18]The undated draft narrative, styled "In the Circuit Court of the U.S. in & for the District of New Jersey, In ejectment for Lands in New Jersey," is in CadP, box 136, folder 6. John Redman Coxe to Tench Coxe, Oct. 27, 1803, CFP, box 66, folder 8.

[19]Coxe to Tilghman and Du Ponceau, Dec. 23, 1803 (retained copy), CFP, box 66, folder 11, to which Du Ponceau replied on the same day assuring Coxe that it "will be immediately attended to." Ibid.

[20]Writs of error, for all practical purposes abolished today in appellate practice, were used as a means of obtaining Supreme Court review of a Circuit Court decision, and in a technical sense should be distinguished from taking an appeal. See *United States v. Goodwin*, 11 U.S. (7 Cranch) 108 (1812).

[21]*Maxfield's Lessee v. Levy*, 4 U.S. (4 Dall.) at 334. The evolution of ejectment as an adaptable fiction is traced in England in J. H. Baker, *An Introduction to English Legal History*, 3rd ed. (London: Butterworths, 1990), 341–43, and in America in Friedman, *History of American Law*, xv.

title controversies. The pleading in this case stated that "John Den a Citizen of the State of Pennsylvania complains of Rebecca Coxe McIlvaine . . . That whereas John Redman Coxe a citizen of the State of Pennsylvania on the second day of January in the year of our Lord 1803 at Trenton in the County of Hunterdon, & within the New Jersey district had demised granted & to farm let to the aforesaid John Den one messuage & tenement, one house, one garden and two hundred acres of Land" for a term of fourteen years and that "the said Rebecca Coxe McIlvaine on the 3d day of January the same month, with force & arms entered into the tenements aforesaid . . . and ejected drove out & removed the said John Den from his farm, his said Term not being yet ended & kept out and still keeps out the said John Den so ejected drove out & removed from his said possession."

John Den, a fictitious stand-in for Daniel Coxe and his son, took paper possession of the premises fictitiously leased to him. Rebecca Coxe McIlvaine, who was drafted as surrogate for the Tench Coxe side, never displaced John Den or anybody else from the premises, and certainly not by "force & arms." Such an elaborate charade was necessary, however, to place at issue the status of Daniel Coxe, who, the special verdict recited, had "before the day of the demise within mentioned conveyed by fit & proper assurances all his right title & Estate in the lands tenements & hereditaments & real Estate which were of Rebecca Coxe late of Trenton . . . to John Redman Coxe, the Lessor of the Plaintiff within named."[22]

Twelve jurors were named in the special verdict as charged with ascertaining the facts, but in reality the only function they performed was a predetermined one—to ratify in formulaic language the statements that the parties had previously agreed on to establish or rebut Daniel Coxe's status as an alien. The special verdict concluded with the jurors disclaiming any judgment on the issue whether "the said Rebecca Coxe McIlvaine is guilty in law of the trespass & ejectment aforesaid or not," praying "the advice of the Court here."[23]

The two judges sitting on circuit acted on the spot without hearing any testimony or argument and giving, Griffith told Tench Coxe, "no manner of opinion—but ordered judgment for the plaintiff [i.e., Daniel Coxe]—as for form sake to bring the point up to the S. Court."[24] Yet, if they took only a moment to confer before

---

[22] The special verdict consists of seven manuscript pages entitled "Pleas before the Judges of the Circuit Court of the United States for the third Circuit, at Trenton, of the Term of October in the Year of our Lord one thousand eight hundred and three—witness the Honorable Bushrod Washington & Robert Morris Esquires, Judges," as bearing a final date of April 3, 1804, and found in CadP, box 157, folder 5. The formal structure for an action in ejectment is set forth on pages 1–2 of the special verdict.

[23] The names of the twelve jurors and their findings occupy pages 2–7 of the special verdict. Whether empanelled in any formal sense or not, the twelve men named as jurors were not fictitious persons. Prior to 1801, Sylvester Doyle was the proprietor of the Bull's Head Tavern in Trenton, as Joseph Broadhurst likewise was the proprietor of the City Tavern; Thomas Potter and William Potts, two other members of the jury, were among prosperous Trentonians who founded the Trenton Water Works at the beginning of the nineteenth century. Walker et al., *History of Trenton*, 319, 325, 370–71n8.

[24] Griffith to Coxe, Friday, postmarked and docketed Apr. 6, 1804, CFP, box 66, folder 7.

announcing their decision, the judges may have been influenced by considerations outside the record. To hold against Daniel Coxe on the allegations set forth in the special verdict would have entailed a more careful inquiry and reasoned judgment than they were prepared to make, or that counsel appearing before them invited the court to make. It is also not impossible that they reacted to the disclosed presence of Tench Coxe as the driving force on the other side.

The next stop, which both parties had deliberately aimed at reaching, was the Supreme Court of the United States.

5

The Supreme Court, 1805

For the Supreme Court, holding improvised sessions in Washington, the nation's new rough-hewn capital, represented a considerable comedown from the more spacious quarters allocated to the Court in Philadelphia during the last decade of the eighteenth century. There, the Supreme Court met in the newly constructed City Hall adjoining the State House, whereas in Washington it was forced to squeeze into a committee room located on the ground floor of the Capitol.[1] Yet, notwithstanding the Court's changed circumstances, in one respect very little had changed. The advocates who appeared before the Court in Philadelphia were the same ones who now appeared before the Court in Washington, as the practice of appellate advocacy continued to be dominated by members of the Philadelphia bar.

In the nostalgic recollection of one of these Philadelphia lawyers, Peter Du Ponceau, it was "always a scene of triumph" when they entered the courtroom in Washington, to be greeted by Justice Bushrod Washington with the accolade, "This is my bar." Du Ponceau wrote of the preferential treatment the delegation from Philadelphia received: "Our causes had a preference over all others, in consideration of the distance we had to travel. The greatest liberality was shown to us, by the members of the profession, who usually attended the court. It was really a proud thing at that time, to be a *Philadelphia lawyer*."[2]

The litigants in the case of *McIlvaine v. Coxe's Lessee* turned to this elite group for representation. Tench Coxe took the altogether natural step of engaging his cousin William Tilghman, a distinguished and successful lawyer, to argue the appeal on behalf of the plaintiff in error (i.e., the party seeking to reverse the decision below). Tilghman would serve briefly as a Philadelphia Common Pleas judge before Thomas McKean in 1806 appointed him Chief Justice of the Pennsylvania Supreme Court, a position he held for twenty-one years.[3]

Tilghman was responsible for persuading Jared Ingersoll to second him as counsel for Coxe. "Mr. Ingersoll will argue your cause," Tilghman wrote Coxe. "I have told him that he shall have $300 paid him, before he leaves Town, for

---

[1] For the Court's location in Washington, see Oliver Wendell Holmes Devise (hereafter Holmes Devise), vol. 2, George Lee Haskins and Herbert A. Johnson, *History of the Supreme Court of the United States: Foundations of Power: John Marshall 1801–15* (New York: Macmillan, 1981), 79–82. Franz Jantzen, of the Office of the Curator, Supreme Court of the United States, has described as "nomadic" the sessions of the Court held in the early part of the nineteenth century; the Court probably occupied the committee room on the ground floor of the Capitol for the 1805 argument in *McIlvaine*, although moving to space on the second floor for the concluding round of argument in 1808. E-mail message from Jantzen to author, Nov. 23, 2015.

[2] Letter of Du Ponceau to Thomas I. Wharton, June 3, 1837, as an appendix to Wharton's memorial essay for William Rawle, published in *Memoirs of the Historical Society of Pennsylvania*, vol. 4, pt. 1 (Philadelphia: M'Carty & Davis, 1840), 86.

[3] Tilghman was another of John Adams's "Midnight Judges." Turner, "The Midnight Judges," *University of Pennsylvania Law Review* 109 (1961): 507–10; and for Tilghman generally, see Charles P. Keith, *The Provincial Councillors of Pennsylvania Who Held Office Between 1733 and 1776 . . . and Their Descendants* (Philadelphia: W. S. Sharp Printing Co., 1883), 409–12.

his fee."[4] Ingersoll had impressive credentials as an advocate and public servant. A member of the Constitutional Convention of 1787, Pennsylvania's first attorney general, and the U.S. attorney for the eastern district of Pennsylvania, he had argued two seminal cases before the Supreme Court in its first decade, both of which found him on the losing side.[5]

For the defendant in error (i.e., the party seeking to uphold the decision below), William Rawle would join Richard Stockton in defending Daniel Coxe's right to inherit before the Supreme Court. In addition to his professional standing, there were connections to the past accounting for the choice of Rawle. His stepfather had been Samuel Shoemaker, mayor of Philadelphia before the Revolution, who in spite of his birthright Quaker status actively supported the British cause by serving with Daniel Coxe as a police magistrate during the British occupation of Philadelphia. Upon the British leaving Philadelphia, Shoemaker retreated to New York City, accompanied by his wife and William Rawle. There Rawle entered the study of the law as an apprentice of John Tabor Kempe, New York's former attorney general and the husband of Grace Coxe Kempe, who was Daniel Coxe's sister and the other party in this proceeding opposing Tench Coxe. Rawle completed his legal studies at the Middle Temple in London, whereupon he returned to Philadelphia and discarded whatever loyalist tendencies he may have had to become a strong Federalist and a respected member of the bar. Yet this branch of the Coxe family might have regarded as a recommendation the past that Rawle had determined to put behind him.[6]

In need of briefing on the intricacies of New Jersey law, Tilghman outlined to Coxe the questions he wished William Griffith to answer, and Coxe immediately applied to Griffith for a response. Of the five questions propounded, the first is an example of the ammunition Tilghman thought his opponents might be trying to assemble: "1st were any laws ever passed in your state enabling aliens generally, or any particular alien or aliens by their names or any class of aliens by description or designation to acquire, hold or sell lands. If so be pleased briefly to give their purport, dates titles, &c."

Griffith promptly replied with specific, detailed answers. On that first question, he wrote that New Jersey had never passed a general naturalization act; that it had never admitted any class of aliens, although "a great no. of foreigners (none however being English) have been naturalized by name" under special legislation,

---

[4]Tilghman to Coxe, Jan. 28, 1805, CFP, box 68, folder 11. By reference to http://www.measuringworth .com/, the present purchasing power of Ingersoll's 1805 fee would come to $6,260.

[5]For biographical detail about Ingersoll, see *Dictionary of American Biography* (2004), s.v. "Ingersoll, Jared." The two cases Ingersoll argued and lost were *Chisholm v. Georgia*, 2 U.S. (2 Dall.) 419 (1793), and *Hylton v. United States*, 3 U.S. (3 Dall.) 171 (1796).

[6]T. I. Wharton, "A Memoir of William Rawle, LL.D, President of the Historical Society, &c." published in *Memoirs of the Historical Society of Pennsylvania*, vol. 4. pt. 1 (Philadelphia: M'Carty & Davis, 1840), 35–76; Keith, *Provincial Councillors of Pennsylvania*, 255–57 (s.v. "Sarah Coates Burge," Rawle's wife), and 244–46 for Samuel Shoemaker.

citing the several authorizing acts by date and the name of the alien beneficiary; and that legislation had also been adopted to allow aliens in specified circumstances to prosecute mortgage debts and hold and purchase lands. On another absolutely crucial question, Griffith confirmed his prior opinion: "No doubt ever existed I believe in New Jersey that an alien either before or since the revolution could not acquire title to real Estate in New Jersey."[7]

Tilghman and Ingersoll were in Washington in early February 1805. From the moment of their arrival, they appear to have been deluged with material and suggestions from their client. "Since our arrival here," Tilghman wrote Coxe, "we have received three packets from you containing notes & Papers—Mr. Ingersoll & myself have given them a careful perusal, & shall derive considerable advantage from them." About the composition and the pending business of the Court, Tilghman had this to say:

> The Judges are all here. Judge Johnson took his seat, for the first time today. There are a good many causes on the Docket, so that it is impossible to say when yours will come on. I understand from one of the Judges, that the point on which your case turns, has never been argued, or taken into consideration by the Supreme Court. Whether Mr. Marshall will sit, I know not. He has at present an Interest in the Question, as the Title of the Fairfax Estate, in the purchase of which he was concerned, is finally settled by compromise.[8]

McIlvaine v. Coxe's Lessee came before the Court for three days of argument on Friday and Saturday, February 15 and 16, and Monday, February 18. The 1805 record of the case consists entirely of the arguments of counsel, which take up fifty-five pages of the report. Judge Cranch, as the reporter, felt an explanation was needed for this large investment in argument only: "The importance and interesting nature of the questions involved in this case, it is hoped will apologize for publishing the arguments of counsel before the ultimate decision of the cause."[9]

To present the arguments as completely as they appear in his report, Cranch would have relied of necessity on counsel and the notes they kept of what they

---

[7] Coxe to Griffith, Dec.17, 1804 (Coxe's retained draft), and Griffith to Coxe, Dec. 19, 1804, CFP, box 68, folder 7.

[8] Tilghman to Coxe, Washington, Feb. 6, 1805, CFP, box 68, folder 12. William Johnson was Jefferson's first appointment to the Court. He followed his own lights, as is often reflected in his dissents. See Holmes Devise, vol. 2, Haskins and Johnson, *History of the Supreme Court of the United States*, 389–90.

[9] *McIlvaine v. Coxe's Lessee*, 6 U.S. (2 Cranch) at 280. The arguments in *McIlvaine v. Coxe's Lessee* may be located online at: https://supreme.justia.com/cases/federal/us/6/280/case.html For the dates of argument, see Minutes of the Supreme Court of the United States, National Archives, Washington, Record Group 267, microfilm M-215, roll 1 (hereafter Minutes of Supreme Court); the minutes are recorded in chronological order beginning February 1, 1790.

said.[10] Unrestrained by enforced time limits, the four lawyers roamed over a large field, touching on a multitude of subjects and authorities: the common law, as recognized in England and America; natural law and justice; history, near and far; *Calvin's Case* and the debated status of the *antenati*; the doctrine of perpetual allegiance; naturalization; the disability of alienage and policy considerations pro and con; the alleged right of expatriation, as distinguished from, or equivalent to, the right of emigration; expatriation as consonant with divine law and the Bible; the measured transition from subject to citizen; dual citizenship; the effective date of independence; treason and attainder; the function of assent in determining allegiance during a revolution, whether explicitly given or necessarily implied; statutory construction; the interpretation of the Treaty of Peace of 1783 and the Jay Treaty of 1794; and the reasoning of philosophers and legal commentators by the score.

William Tilghman led the argument as counsel for Tench Coxe. He stressed the importance of the case by stating what an anonymous member of the Court had earlier confided to him: "The question which arises in this case . . . has never been decided in this court, nor in the State of New Jersey." To be more specific:

> It is, in substance, whether a person born in the U.S. while they were British colonies, and who took no part in favour of the revolution but joined the British army in an early stage of the war, and from that time to this, by the whole tenor of his actions and declarations, has shewn his election not to be a citizen of the U.S. but to adhere to the British empire, was capable of taking land in *New Jersey* by descent in the year 1802.[11]

Tilghman proceeded meticulously to lay out the facts in support of his client's position as incorporated in the special verdict. In his submission, Daniel Coxe never owed natural allegiance to the state of New Jersey; when the Revolution began, he had a right to choose his side, and all the evidence pointed to his having chosen decisively to align himself with the British cause. True, he may have remained in New Jersey for an interval after the state passed an act on October 4, 1776, declaring that all persons then "abiding" there were duty bound to adhere to the new government, but the objective of that legislation, as Tilghman saw it, was simply to deter persons from joining the enemy during the war, which

---

[10] William Cranch, still one more "Midnight Judge," was appointed under separate legislation for the District of Columbia Circuit Court; Cranch survived in office for the astonishing period of fifty-four years. Although he served as an unpaid reporter for the Supreme Court from 1801 through 1815, both the Court and practitioners in front of it became critical of what one author has charitably described as Cranch's "vagaries," including inaccuracies in reporting the arguments of counsel and chronic tardiness in completing his work. Holmes Devise, vol. 2, Haskins and Johnson, *History of the Supreme Court of the United States*, 497; and see Craig Joyce, "The Rise of the Supreme Court Reporter: An Institutional Perspective on Marshall Court Ascendancy," *Michigan Law Review* 83 (1985): 1306–12.

[11] 6 U.S. (2 Cranch) at 280.

did not make them committed citizens. If, however, Daniel Coxe acquired by force of that statute a temporary allegiance to New Jersey, nothing could prevent him after the Treaty of Peace in 1783, the beginning of a new era, from leaving the country and transferring his allegiance "where he pleased," which brought Tilghman to the core question in this case concerning the right of expatriation, for Coxe had provided a cumulative, consistent record of presenting himself not as a citizen of New Jersey but as a subject of the British crown. "Of all people the Americans are the last," Tilghman declaimed, "to call in question the right of expatriation. They have derived infinite advantage from its exercise by others who have left Europe and settled here. It is denied by the constitution of no state, nor of the United States."[12]

Tilghman turned to a critical precedent in English law that both sides in the appeal to the Supreme Court had to grapple with. *Calvin's Case* was decided in 1608 by an extraordinary array of English judges, headed by Lord Chief Justice Edward Coke.[13] The particular question in that case was whether a child born in 1603 in Scotland after James VI of Scotland had become James I of England could take title to land in England or was barred from doing so as an alien. In extended analysis, drawing on a variety of sources, the court ruled that Calvin (his actual name was "Colville"), as *"postnatus,"* born after the accession of James I, was a subject of the English crown notwithstanding his birth in Scotland.

Though not directly at issue, Coke also addressed the status of the *"antenati,"* those born in Scotland before the date of James's accession to the English throne, holding that the *antenati* owed permanent allegiance by their birth to James, as king of Scotland, and were therefore aliens under English law. It was this second aspect of *Calvin's Case*, suggesting an indissoluble bond conferred by birth, which Tench Coxe's lawyers sought to overcome in their attempt to defeat Daniel Coxe's claim to share in his aunt's estate. Having been born in New Jersey well before the Revolution, did Daniel Coxe thereby acquire permanent allegiance not simply to the colony of his birth but to whatever successor power might take office?

For Tilghman, *Calvin's Case* was determined "when the ideas of the royal prerogative were extravagant and absurd." That the constitution of New Jersey may have provided for the acceptance of the common law of England did not mean accepting "those parts which were inconvenient, or inconsistent with our situation—such as that the king can do no wrong—personal and perpetual allegiance, &c." Moreover, the New Jersey constitution was "at variance with the principle of the *antenati*, which is founded on the basis that natural allegiance

---

[12] 6 U.S. (2 Cranch) at 286.

[13] *Calvin's Case*, 7 Coke Report 1a, 77 ER 377 (K.B. 1608). See Kettner, *American Citizenship*, 16–28; Polly J. Price, "Natural Law and Birthright Citizenship in *Calvin's Case* (1608)," *Yale Journal of Law & the Humanities* 9 (1997): 73–145.

cannot be shaken off; whereas the constitution of New Jersey declares that protection and allegiance are reciprocal."[14]

Tilghman ended by summarizing the appellant's position: Daniel Coxe was always a subject of the king of Great Britain and never a subject or citizen of the state of New Jersey; but if, by force, he became a subject of New Jersey, he had the right to shake off that compulsory allegiance and return to his natural allegiance as soon as the force ceased, which happened upon the Treaty of Peace; so that, under all circumstances, he must be viewed as an alien incapable of taking lands in New Jersey by descent.[15]

When the Court convened the next morning at eleven o'clock, William Rawle rose as counsel for Daniel Coxe. No more than Tilghman did he hold back in developing at length the case for his client, which, judging by the minutes, took all of the Court's Saturday session. He began by stating that the title of John Redman Coxe as lessor was good unless his father, Daniel Coxe, was incapable of taking by descent from his aunt either because he was an alien or because he had been attainted of treason in New Jersey during the Revolution. The jurors rendering the special verdict had ruled out the latter disability, leaving for the Supreme Court to decide the single issue of alienage.[16]

Rawle put before the Court three propositions: that every inhabitant of a state became at the Declaration of Independence a citizen of such state; that, owing allegiance to such state, he acquired the capacity to take and hold real estate in it; and that of this allegiance he could not divest himself, nor could he be deprived of this capacity except as punishment for crimes. But, to take the first proposition, did the Declaration of Independence bind everyone, even those who wished to continue as loyal subjects of the king? Rawle contended that, though the Declaration was not a unanimous act, it was the act of a majority binding on the minority. According to Rawle, "This principle was never questioned. The minority were never considered *aliens*. Hence the penal laws of that time made by the states consider some of that minority as *traitors*."

So far the logic of Rawle's argument would suggest that the minority was forced into submission, however strongly individual members might protest their

---

[14] 6 U.S. (2 Cranch) at 289–90.

[15] 6 U.S. (2 Cranch) at 291–92.

[16] 6 U.S. (2 Cranch) at 292. The special verdict recited the inquisition in New Jersey leading to the forfeiture of all of Daniel's Coxe's real and personal property in the state as a consequence of his joining the British in Philadelphia "against the form of his allegiance to the State of New Jersey, and against the peace of the same." By way of contrast, however, the special verdict referred to the proceeding in Pennsylvania against Coxe personally, who was attainted for treason in that state. That Daniel Coxe's counsel regarded this as a critical point of differentiation is borne out by the fact that the record before the Supreme Court consisted of three documents: the writ of error, the special verdict, and an exemplified record of the full inquisition proceeding in New Jersey, dated Dec. 11, 1778, as certified on Jan. 7, 1805. Appellate Cases of the United States Supreme Court, 1792–1831, National Archives, Washington, Record Group 267, microfilm M-214, roll 7, Case No. 182.

adherence to the king. Yet, Rawle tried to have it both ways: "To this distinguished act in the history of man [i.e., the Declaration], the *assent* of the people was essential." Granting that the language of the Declaration had governments "deriving their just Powers from the Consent of the Governed," he produced a circular definition of *essential assent* as being "implied from the assent of the *majority*," which could "only be known by the assent of the states."[17]

Rawle traced the course New Jersey took in exercising its independence. It may have been the first state to adopt a new constitution and a new form of government on July 2, 1776, enfranchising "*inhabitants*, who have resided in the county for 12 months, and who had property to a certain value. Thus the *inhabitants*, without distinction, are made members of the society, *citizens* of the state. Being citizens, all the rights of *acquiring* and *enjoying* property attached to them." On October 4, 1776, the New Jersey assembly passed a law providing that every person "abiding" within the state, and deriving protection from its laws, was a member of the state and owed allegiance to it. "*Daniel Coxe* did at that time *abide* within the state; he therefore *owed allegiance* to it, and was a *member* of it," and nothing the special verdict detailed his doing subsequently deprived him of that status. The forfeiture proceedings against him in New Jersey authorized seizure of his property for joining the British in breach of his allegiance but did not constitute a judgment against him personally as a condemned traitor.[18]

Counsel for both parties acknowledged the importance of *Respublica v. Chapman*, a Pennsylvania case decided, as William Tilghman remarked, "in the very heat of the Revolution," and often cited in the postwar era to determine under what circumstances a person might safely opt out of the Revolution and declare allegiance to the king.[19] How much time would a loyal subject of the king be granted after the Declaration to make up his mind, and what act or acts would establish his election before he found himself bound as a citizen for having "abided" too long in a newly formed state?

Chief Justice McKean confronted those questions when, in a 1781 trial, he instructed a jury called on to decide whether Samuel Chapman was guilty of treason. Born in Bucks County, Chapman remained there until December 26, 1776, when he left Pennsylvania and joined the British forces. Some time later he was captured, taken into custody as a prisoner of war, and charged with treason under the Pennsylvania attainder statute. Chapman's defense was that he had never been a subject or inhabitant of the Commonwealth of Pennsylvania, having left the state before a government had come into existence to which he owed a duty of allegiance. His counsel argued that on December 26, the date of Chapman's departure:

---

[17] 6 U.S. (2 Cranch) at 292–94. Italicized words or phrases appear as such throughout in quoted material.
[18] 6 U.S. (2 Cranch) at 294–96.
[19] 1 U.S. (1 Dall.) 53 (Pa. 1781). For Tilghman quote, see 6 U.S. (2 Cranch) at 284.

> There was no government established in Pennsylvania, from which he could receive protection; and consequently, there was none to which he could owe allegiance—protection and allegiance being political obligations of a reciprocal nature. The doctrine of perpetual allegiance, to be found in the books, applies only to established and settled governments; not to the case of withdrawing from an old government, and erecting a distinct one. Then, every member of the community has a right of election, or resort to which he pleases; and even after the new system is formed, he is entitled to express his dissent; and dissenting from a majority, to retire with impunity into another country.[20]

In what was reported "a learned and circumstantial charge," McKean guided the jury to a verdict of acquittal, but by a circuitous route. McKean told the jurors that, "a kind of government, independent of Great Britain, was administered in Pennsylvania, antecedent to the establishment of the present constitution [in September 1776]." Moreover, a formal compact was not "a necessary foundation of government," not when a council of safety and other committees existed "to secure, as far as so imperfect a system could, the rights of life, liberty and property within this state."[21]

Having rejected the argument that Chapman had left the state at a time when a government had not yet emerged in Pennsylvania sufficient to compel his allegiance, McKean nevertheless reflected on the nature of the still continuing revolutionary conflict in a passage that would be frequently quoted: "In *civil wars* every man chuses his party; but generally that side which prevails, arrogates the right of treating those who are vanquished as rebels." If the voice of the majority must ultimately prevail in forming a new government, he took it as a given that "the minority have, individually, an unrestrainable right to remove with their property into another country; that a reasonable time for that purpose ought to be allowed; and, in short, that none are subjects of the adopted government, who have not freely assented to it."[22]

Fortunately for Chapman, and for McKean, too, who had rather painted himself into a corner, the Pennsylvania legislature had passed a treason statute on February 11, 1777, describing those from whom allegiance was due as "persons *then* inhabiting the state, or who should *thereafter* become its inhabitants." Accordingly, by legislative action, the cutoff date was advanced to the date of the treason statute, and Chapman could be acquitted.[23]

---

[20] 1 U.S. (1 Dall.) at 53.

[21] 1 U.S. (1 Dall.) at 55–57.

[22] 1 U.S. (1 Dall.) at 58.

[23] 1 U.S. (1 Dall.) at 58–59. A further complication arose relating to the subsequently enacted attainder statute and its possible retroactive effect, which McKean, in his instruction to the jury, disposed of by adroit statutory interpretation. 1 U.S. (1 Dall.) at 59–60.

Representing the Tench Coxe side, Tilghman relied on McKean in *Chapman's* case to establish that, at this early stage in the Revolution, every person had a right to choose his side, which he argued Daniel Coxe had done by demonstrably going over to the British side.[24] Representing Daniel Coxe, Rawle had no trouble, on the other hand, in distinguishing his client's position from Chapman's. "Chapman left Pennsylvania the 26th of December, 1776; Coxe [left New Jersey] not till September 1777." Daniel Coxe was an inhabitant of the state of New Jersey on October 4, 1776, when a declaratory law was enacted similar to the Pennsylvania statute of February 11, 1777. Had Samuel Chapman been a resident of Pennsylvania on February 11, he, like Daniel Coxe in New Jersey at the earlier date, would have been locked into citizenship and subject to punishment for treason.[25]

The balance of Rawle's argument was devoted to refuting the idea that Coxe had divested himself of his allegiance to New Jersey in the exercise of a supposed right of expatriation. Rawle denied that any such unilateral right existed, and that, even if it did, the various activities attributed to Daniel Coxe in the special verdict amounted to an unequivocal renunciation of his citizenship:

> Our opponents have piled together a confused and shapeless mass of evidence, on which this court cannot act. Since even if expatriation had been allowed by the constitution or laws of New Jersey, all the different facts put together would not amount to the technical fact of expatriation, and since if expatriation be not allowed, they are of no more importance than finding whether Mr. Coxe wore a blue coat or a brown one.[26]

Rawle pointed out what he conceived was a basic inconsistency in the argument for the appellant: "The counsel contend for the rigid doctrine, peculiar to *feudal tenures*, that an alien cannot hold land, and yet discard the more rational concomitant feudal principle, which has been engrafted into the common law, that *nemo potest exuere patriam*."[27]

In its session on Monday, February 18, the Court heard first from Richard Stockton for Daniel Coxe and then from Jared Ingersoll for Tench Coxe. It must be assumed that co-counsel for each party had conferred and allocated between them separate responsibility for developing a particular line of argument. Stockton focused on the place of birth as determining "the condition of the subject . . . because he there receives the protection necessary to the preservation of life, during

---

[24] *McIlvaine v. Coxe's Lessee*, 6 U.S. (2 Cranch) at 284–85.

[25] 6 U.S. (2 Cranch) at 300. Rawle erred, maybe deliberately for the purpose of this argument, in having Daniel Coxe leave New Jersey as late as September 1777. In his memorial and testimony to the Loyalist Claims Commission, Coxe stated that, under the threat of hostilities, he and his family relocated to near Philadelphia early in December 1776, where they remained "secluded on the Schuilkill [*sic*] till the British Army came to Philadelphia." Memorial of Daniel Coxe, March 13, 1784, and Evidence, Nov. 29, 1784, AO 12/13/181–83, 202.

[26] 6 U.S. (2 Cranch) at 301.

[27] 6 U.S. (2 Cranch) at 306. The doctrine of perpetual allegiance: "No man can renounce his own country."

the helpless years of infancy." It followed as a bedrock principle of the common law that "no man born a subject can be an alien," even though "a change of sovereigns should take place, and distinct government be formed." So Coke had held in *Calvin's Case* when he ruled that the *antenati* of Scotland could not take by descent in England after the accession of James to the English throne since at the time of their birth they were aliens in England. Nothing in the common law, however, prevented emigration to another country, to "a more genial clime," as Stockton put it, so long as it is understood that, "if you do emigrate, you shall still retain *the privileges* and be under the restraints of your natural allegiance."[28]

If the place of birth did not conclusively fix the status of Daniel Coxe, then Stockton reverted to the prior argument of Rawle about the effect of Coxe's "abiding" in New Jersey as making him a member of a new community. Stockton deemed it important as Rawle had done to refute the contention that Coxe had been stripped of his citizenship by the proceedings against him resulting in the forfeiture of his property in New Jersey. The object of the legislature in authorizing the confiscation of all the real and personal property of the offending subject was not so much to punish transgressions "as to bring money into the treasury." The legislature had refrained from following the example of its sister state, Pennsylvania, in declining to pass attainder acts affecting the person of the offender, deeming such acts unfair in that "they take the life of a man without trial by jury— [convicting] him of personal offenses in his absence, against a maxim of the law."[29]

Stockton was also at pains to counter the notion that Daniel Coxe on his own had expatriated himself. Stockton saw reliance on that concept—he called it a "modern theory"—as all that remained of the appellant's case. Under the common law, "expatriation is not barely not permitted, but it is *distinctly prohibited*." By its constitution, New Jersey accepted the common law of England generally, "except such parts as are inconsistent with the rights and privileges of that charter." Opposing counsel invoked that exception in an attempt to overcome the doctrine of perpetual allegiance. "I am at a loss," Stockton said, "to discover how perpetual allegiance to the government established in New Jersey with the authority of the people can be inconsistent with the rights of that charter which created and set in motion that very government."[30]

During this concluding day of argument, Both Stockton and Jared Ingersoll, who would follow, sought to gain the attention of the Court by rhetorical flourishes, which Judge Cranch, preparing his report at some distance in time from the courtroom appearance of counsel, managed to preserve or embellish. After Stockton enumerated the several laws adopted by the state of New Jersey in the revolutionary period, he provides this example of an attention-getting flourish:

---

[28] 6 U.S. (2 Cranch) at 309–11.
[29] 6 U.S. (2 Cranch) at 312–14.
[30] 6 U.S. (2 Cranch) at 316.

We see an old government dissolved and a new one created. The people at first, and their representatives afterwards, declare by law *all men abiding within* their territory, subjects of the new government. They pass treason acts, define allegiance, and enforce its duties by the accustomed sanctions of the law. These laws operated on D[aniel] C[oxe]. He was an *abider* within their territory. They claim him as a subject, and punish him for refusing to yield obedience. Shall, then, this same government, which with a voice of thunder proclaimed him a subject and punished him as one, or shall an individual under its law say to him, you are an *alien*? Shall he be declared a *subject* to punish him and an *alien* to punish him? A *subject* to take all he has and an *alien* to prevent his acquiring any in the future? Shall he be made poor by *citizenship*, and be kept poor *for want of it*?[31]

In his opening on behalf of Tench Coxe, Jared Ingersoll refused to be upstaged:

The doctrines advanced upon the present occasion are, to me, *novel, strange, and alarming*. That the *postnati*, against whom we have no cause of complaint, should be excluded, while the *antenati* are preferred who injured us. That the French who aided us are called aliens, while the British royalist refugee may hold land as a citizen, is a language I do not understand. If the law is so, it is strange, and I must abandon an idea I have always cherished, that the rules of law were founded in sound sense.[32]

Ingersoll got straight to the point in asking "a question of magnitude," and that is whether Daniel Coxe could expatriate himself and become a subject of the king of Great Britain. "This is," he noted, "a new case in the history of nations, to which the little case of *Calvin*, the Scotchman, bears no proportion." When the authority of the crown was rejected, "the inhabitants of the former colonies were so far in a state of nature, that each man was at liberty to choose his side—remain a *subject*, or become a *citizen*. This interval of election continued until new systems of government were formed, adopted, and organized, after which period, (not previously) residence was an implied assent to the fortunes and destinies of the United States." Ingersoll found direct support in McKean's instructions to the jury "in the memorable case of *Chapman*, the British light-horseman, charged with treason." But once the right of election had passed, "the right of expatriation succeeded."[33]

Ingersoll correctly summarized the analysis of Rawle, who had insisted that the right of expatriation was not to be equated with the right of free movement, of emigration; the former, Rawle had argued, was of municipal regulation, whereas the latter, a natural right, meaning that, although emigration cannot be restrained,

---

[31] 6 U.S. (2 Cranch) at 314–15.
[32] 6 U.S. (2 Cranch) at 321.
[33] 6 U.S. (2 Cranch) at 321–23.

expatriation requires the consent of the government. Ingersoll made light of this distinction as finding no sanction in the law and being "the offspring of [Rawle's] creative imagination." For Ingersoll, "*emigration* is to be understood as co-extensive with *expatriation*," and yet in his search for support, he lacked solid authority in the law books, invoking instead divine law, the law of nature, the law of nations, and when all else failed, the Bible: "the most venerable book of antiquity [where] we find expatriation practised, approved, and never restrained. The family of Jacob became subjects to the Egyptian monarch, Moses abandoned Egypt, his native land, and David left Saul, his prince."[34]

Whether an individual possessed the right of expatriation was not an entirely new question for the Supreme Court. It had come before the Court, sitting in Philadelphia, in *Talbot v. Jansen*,[35] a prize case involving a ship captured by an American citizen who attempted to renounce his American citizenship in order to take a commission from France as a privateer. In opinions delivered seriatim, Justice Iredell found this ruse a "palpable violation of our own law . . . as well as of the law of nations generally," relieving the Court of the necessity of ruling on the claimed exercise of a right of expatriation. Yet, alone among his colleagues on the bench, he couldn't resist voicing a personal view on expatriation:

> This involves the great question as to the right of expatriation, upon which so much has been said in this cause. Perhaps it is not necessary it should be explicitly decided on this occasion: but I shall freely express my sentiments on the subject. That a man ought not to be a slave; that he ought not be confined against his will to a particular spot, because he happened to draw his first breath upon it; that he should not be compelled to continue in a society to which he is accidentally attached, when he can better his situation elsewhere, much less when he must starve in one country, and may live comfortably in another; are positions which I hold as strongly as any man, and they are such as most nations in the world appear clearly to recognize.[36]

Murray v. The Charming Betsy,[37] another prize case, also raised the issue of expatriation; and once again the Supreme Court, speaking through Chief Justice Marshall, maneuvered around it. *The Charming Betsy*, originally an American-built ship, was sold in St. Thomas to Jared Shattuck, who, though born in Connecticut, went to St. Thomas as an infant, where he carried on trade as a

---

[34] 6 U.S. (2 Cranch) at 323–24.

[35] 3 U.S. (3 Dall.) 133 (1795).

[36] 3 U.S. (3 Dall.) at 161–62 (1795). Justice Cushing in his concurring opinion in this case shied away from reaching any decision concerning the doctrine of expatriation, preferring instead to view, in "a very narrow compass," the "facts in this case, so far as they appear to me to be essential to forming an opinion." 3 U.S. (3 Dall.) at 168–69. He would take much the same tack thirteen years later in delivering the Court's opinion attributed to his authorship in *McIlvaine v. Coxe's Lessee*. 8 U.S. (4 Cranch) 209 (1808).

[37] 6 U.S. (2 Cranch) 64 (1804).

Danish subject, married, and swore an oath of allegiance to the Danish crown. Intercepted in trade in the Caribbean, first by a French privateer and then by an American frigate commanded by Captain Murray, *The Charming Betsy* proceeded to port in Philadelphia as an American prize vessel engaged in illicit trade with France under the nonintercourse law of 1800; there the Danish consul claimed it as the property of a Danish subject. From a decision of the federal district court upholding the legality of Captain Murray's seizure, an appeal was taken to the Supreme Court.

John Marshall declined the invitation of Murray's counsel to find Shattuck an American citizen engaged in illicit trade by relying on the doctrine of perpetual allegiance. Nor did he need to rule on the right of expatriation: "Whether a person born in the United States or becoming the citizen according to the established laws of the country can divest himself absolutely of that character otherwise than in such a manner as may be prescribed by law is a question which it is not necessary at present to decide." The Chief Justice cited as an important principle that "an act of Congress ought never to be construed to violate the law of nations if any other possible construction remains," which led him to decide that, American citizen or not, by becoming a "Danish burgher" Shattuck had removed himself from the protection of the United States and the category of persons whose property under the statute was subject to seizure.[38]

In 1805 the Supreme Court consisted of six members, but only four of them— Justices Cushing, Paterson, Washington, and Johnson— were recorded as participating in *McIlvaine v. Coxe's Lessee*. Justice Samuel Chase was absent because the Senate had yet to vote on articles of impeachment filed against him.[39] When William Tilghman left for Washington to represent Tench Coxe, he was uncertain what Chief Justice Marshall's role might be. According to Judge Cranch's report, Marshall "did not sit in this cause," stating as the reason that he had "formed a decided opinion on the principal question, where his interest was concerned."[40]

How and when Marshall might have signaled his withdrawal can only be surmised. The minutes of the Supreme Court show him sitting at these sessions, which, although contrary to present practice, is not inconsistent with his removing himself from the case. He had a good, if not compelling, reason to withdraw in *McIlvaine* because of his stake in the seemingly endless litigation over the Fairfax estate in Virginia. The title to a tract of valuable land that John Marshall and his brother James acquired, as part of a syndicate, from Denny Martin, a nephew

---

[38] 6 U.S. (2 Cranch) at 118–21. Though at the time of his 1805 argument in *McIlvaine v. Coxe's Lessee*, Jared Ingersoll could not refer to a published report of Marshall's opinion in *The Charming Betsy*, he misrepresented the holding by stating that in that decision "expatriation was expressly recognized . . . as operating the extinguishment of the previous character of citizen of the United States." 6 U.S. (2 Cranch) at 329.

[39] He was acquitted on March 1, 1805. For an account of Chase's impeachment and trial, see Holmes Devise, vol. 2, Haskins and Johnson, *History of the Supreme Court of the United States*, 223–45.

[40] 6 U.S. (2 Cranch) at 280 (annotation by Judge Cranch at the bottom of the opening page).

of Lard Fairfax, would have been vulnerable had Martin been determined an alien; a compromise settlement reached with the Commonwealth of Virginia in 1796 did not entirely eliminate a risk that continued until the Supreme Court finally disposed of the matter in two related decisions in 1813 and 1816.[41]

To the disappointment of Tench Coxe, who, in the absence of any news from Washington, had written Tilghman and Ingersoll on February 24, "We are extremely anxious to have the cause argued, I hope nothing will prevent it," the Court indicated that it was presently unable to render a decision in *McIlvaine v. Coxe's Lessee* and put the matter over for future consideration.[42] On his return to Philadelphia, Tilghman sent Coxe a brief note, "I got home last night. Your cause was argued, but we suppose that Judgment will not be given before the next Term. It is conjectured that the Court do not agree in opinion."[43]

---

[41] For Marshall's interest in the ongoing litigation concerning the Fairfax estate, see Charles F. Hobson, "John Marshall and the Fairfax Litigation: The Background of *Martin v. Hunter's Lessee*," *Journal of Supreme Court History 1996*, vol. 2, 36–50. The Supreme Court (Marshall abstaining) acted to confirm the title of the Marshalls in *Fairfax's Devisee v. Hunter's Lessee*, 11 U.S. (7 Cranch) 603 (1813), and then to reaffirm its constitutional right to decide in *Martin v. Hunter's Lessee*, 14 U.S. (1 Wheat.) 304 (1816).

[42] Coxe to Tilghman and Ingersoll, Feb. 24, 1805 (retained copy), CFP, box 68, folder 12.

[43] Tilghman to Coxe, Feb. 28, 1805, CFP, ibid.

6

The Supreme Court, 1808

The failure of the Supreme Court to reach a decision increased tension between Tench Coxe and his brothers. From the outset his brothers were never as committed as he was to denying Daniel Coxe and Grace Kempe any share in their aunt's estate. William Coxe remained on friendly terms with Phineas Bond, the British consul who acted behind the scenes for Daniel Coxe and his son, John Redman Coxe. Not long after his aunt had died, William Coxe acknowledged in a letter to Bond the receipt of a "Pipe of wine . . . in good order" for which he enclosed his check in payment. Rather than focusing on the litigation his brother was plotting, William Coxe took responsibility for the sale of their aunt's house and personal effects in Trenton; he further tried to answer the concerns of tenants and prospective purchasers who were uneasy about the contested title to the considerable land in Rebecca Coxe's name located in New Jersey and New York State.[1]

John D. Coxe, the persnickety presiding judge of the Common Pleas Court in Philadelphia, was understandably anxious to maintain good relations with Chief Justice Edward Shippen, Jr., a Daniel Coxe ally, as well as with John Redman Coxe, a respected Philadelphia physician. Judge Coxe never fully signed on to the litigation, raising from the start various legal questions and objections. It was to him, the "Honorable John D. Coxe," that Daniel Coxe addressed a conciliatory letter from London in November 1802: "In respect to the just expectations that my sister and I conceive to be entitled to as joint heirs with you & the Family in America, as to our late Aunt Rebecca's property Real & personal I have to trust that every liberality may be extended to preserve Family Harmony; and that you will suppress any & every sentiment hostile to it, should any such unfortunately subsist on your side of the water."[2]

Tench Coxe's third brother, Daniel W. Coxe, appears for the most part missing in the family consultations concerning Rebecca Coxe's estate. A busy and successful Philadelphia merchant, he would become engrossed in speculation in Spanish Grant lands in Louisiana, West Florida, and elsewhere. As for any reaction one might attribute to him respecting the family contest over his aunt's estate, he could well have been influenced in his thinking by his marriage to Chief Justice Shippen's granddaughter.[3]

---

[1] William Coxe, Jr., to Phineas Bond, Aug. 27, 1802, CadP, box 206, folder 7. For evidence of William Coxe's principal concerns, see WC to Tench Coxe, Dec. 7, 1803, CFP, box 66, folder 10 (tenant concerns); WC to Tench Coxe, Jan. [2], 1806, CFP, box 70, folder 12 (recommended sale of their aunt's house "in want of considerable repair"); and WC to Tench Coxe, Mar. 4, 1807, CFP, box 73, folder 3 (defining his responsibility as a "general superintendence" over Rebecca Coxe's real estate).

[2] Horace Binney provides a thumbnail portrait of Judge Coxe in Charles Chauncey Binney, *The Life of Horace Binney, With Selection from his Letters* (Philadelphia: J. B. Lippincott, 1903), 41 ("a sound lawyer, and a very honest man, a little too much disturbed by his doubts, and his talent for making distinctions"). Daniel Coxe to Honorable John D. Coxe, London, Nov. 4, 1802, CFP, box 65, folder 2 (partial photocopy of original).

[3] For biographical information about Daniel W. Coxe, see the HSP listing for his papers (Collection 2091) at: http://discover.hsp.org/Record/hsp.ead.at01-2091/Description#tabnav.

Before he initiated suit in *McIlvaine v. Coxe's Lessee*, Tench Coxe's brothers knew about his improvident tendencies. In his will their father gave the three of them their shares in his estate outright, but aware of Tench's propensity to incur indebtedness he could not pay, William Coxe, Sr., put his share in a spendthrift trust, of which two of the trustees were William Coxe, Jr., and Daniel W. Coxe, appointed by their father to monitor Tench's expenditures.[4]

The litigation against Daniel Coxe and Grace Kempe, pursued through the inconclusive result in 1805, had been a financially taxing experience for Tench Coxe. In addition, he now proposed to begin partition proceedings in New York to divide up the land there among Rebecca Coxe's several heirs before the Supreme Court reached its decision and without the joinder of Daniel Coxe and Grace Kempe in the proceeding. To cope with mounting expenses, he sought to obtain contributions from his brothers, only to receive this reply from William Coxe:

> I mentioned to my brothers the idea of lending you the amt. of your advances in the question of Alienage. It was, if I recollect, thought improper to aid by money the presentation of a claim which we had consented to relinquish partly from an opinion that it would be eventually so doubtful as to leave little hope of success. After what passed between my brothers and myself with Mr. Bond and Dr. Coxe it might appear very inconsistent on our part, if not the complection [*sic*] of duplicity. I am however perfectly willing that you should apply to my Brothers and if their consent shell be obtained, mine shall not be refused.[5]

For all of 1806 the parties in *McIlvaine* marked time. Toward the end of that year William Rawle gave notice to Tench Coxe's counsel that the case would be listed for reargument before the Supreme Court in its upcoming February term. William Tilghman no longer acted for Coxe, having assumed his duties as Chief Justice of the Pennsylvania Supreme Court; he would be replaced by Coxe's long-standing legal advisor, Peter Stephen Du Ponceau. The notice from Rawle caught Coxe off guard and precipitated an unpleasant exchange between him and his counsel.

Coxe addressed a letter to Jared Ingersoll and Peter Du Ponceau about the "fees in the Case of McIlvaine & Coxe," which "the candor of your characters"

---

[4] Cooke, *Tench Coxe*, 410–11. William Coxe, Sr., executed a codicil to his will on March 23, 1801, putting Tench Coxe's share of his estate in trust and naming his two sons and his nephew William Tilghman as trustees to ensure repayment of debts Tench Coxe owed the testator and another party. *New Jersey Archives*, 1st ser. "Calendar of New Jersey Wills, Administrations, Etc., 1801–1805" (Trenton, NJ: MacCrellish & Quigley Co., 1946), 39:10

[5] William Coxe, Jr., to Tench Coxe, July 23, 1805, CFP, box 69, folder 9. Nothing came of the proposed partition proceeding because Egbert Benson advised Coxe that a partition would not succeed unless all interested parties joined in the action. Coxe to Benson, June 10, 1805 (retained copy), CFP, box 69, folder 6; Benson to Coxe, Jan. 23, 1806, CFP, box 70, folder 13.

had satisfied him that they would find acceptable. They scarcely could be expected to find acceptable what followed:

> My tenth of Miss R Coxe's estate and a very small Interest of Miss McIlvaine (now Mrs. Joshua M. Wallace Junr.) is all that is concerned in this case, for my brothers all refuse to partake in the discussion or expences. A fee of 300 dollars each & 100 dollars of expences were paid for a full arguing of the cause making 700 dollars upon our little interests. I have had as valuable causes managed by Philadel & interior [?] Supreme Court lawyers for 50 & 100 dollars each in places more distant than Washington City. . . . It would appear to me that a recapitulation of the arguments used before, from the notes of Messrs Ingersol [sic] & Tilghman, with any useful additional matter would be all that would be required, or perhaps acceptible [sic] to the Court. I certainly should think more than one such able counsel as either of you or Messrs Tilghman or Rawle requisite to either side on this occasion, and if you were not all going down on other Causes, I assume that the parties would not extend further than one gentleman each from hence to restate the arguments with any new case or arguments. I offer these Ideas for your friendly consideration, and will have the pleasure to call on you.[6]

This letter prompted an immediate and pointed reply from Du Ponceau and Ingersoll (Figure 3):

> Dear Sir
>
> We have received your favor of yesterday on the subject of our compensation in the Case of McIlvaine v. Coxe. As we have not sought this business, & as discussions on a subject so delicate are always unpleasant to us, we think it best to decline being further concerned in the Cause.
>
> We are respectfully
>
> Dear Sir
>
> Your most obed. humb Servnts
>
> Jared Ingersoll
> Peter S. Du Ponceau[7]

---

[6]Coxe to Ingersoll and Du Ponceau, Jan. 12, 1807 (retained copy), CFP, box 72, folder 13. Coxe is referring to two different Tilghmans—William Tilghman, who had represented him in 1805, and Edward Tilghman, William's cousin, who had replaced Richard Stockton as counsel on the Daniel Coxe side in this second phase of the case. Edward Tilghman had previously been consulted on the advisability of structuring the ejectment action as a diversity suit. He was both the nephew and the son-in-law of Benjamin Chew, the last Chief Justice of Pennsylvania to serve under the crown. Like his cousin William, he studied law at the Middle Temple in London, and also like William, he commanded universal respect in his profession. Keith, *The Provincial Councillors of Pennsylvania*, 336–37 (s.v. "Elizabeth Chew," Edward Tilghman's wife).

[7]Jan. 13, 1807, CFP, box 72, folder 13 (in Du Ponceau's handwriting).

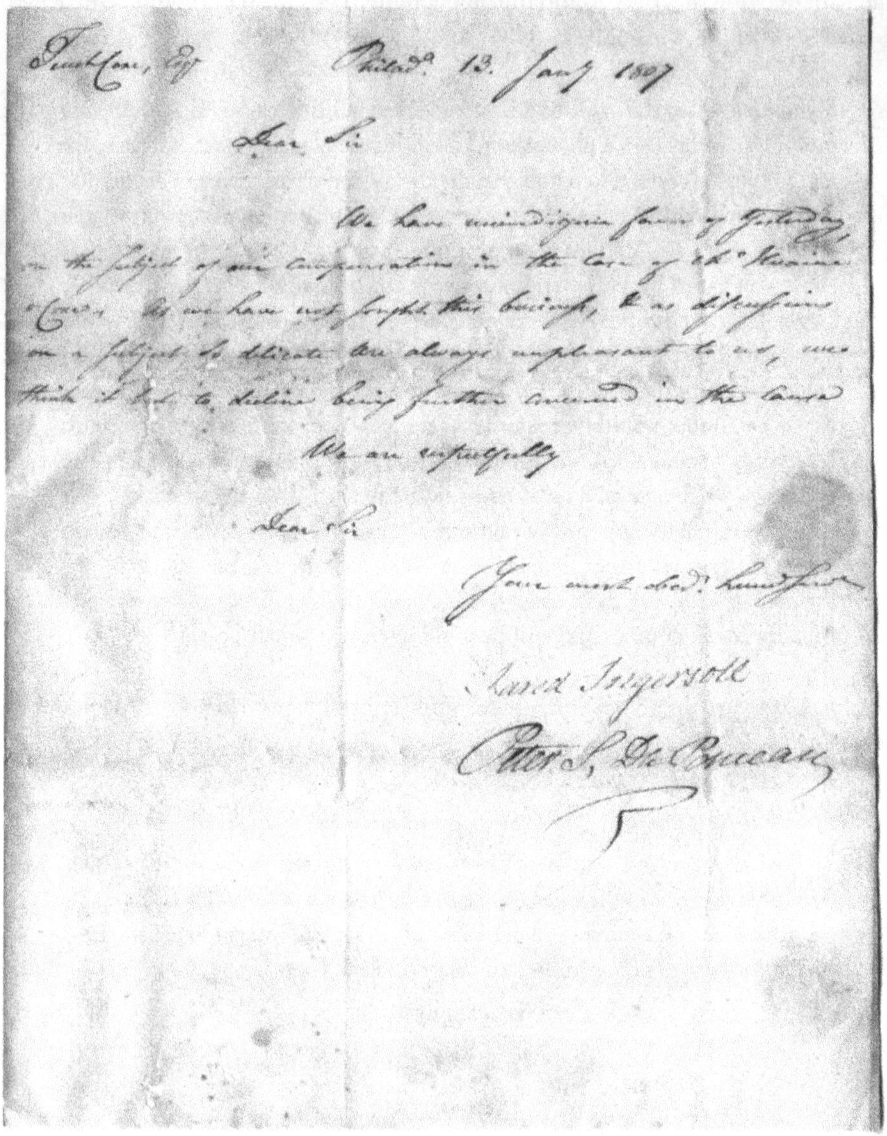

Figure 3.   Letter of Du Ponceau and Ingersoll to Tench Coxe dated Jan. 13, 1807, in the Coxe
Family Papers.

Courtesy of the Historical Society of Pennsylvania.

Meanwhile, William Rawle assumed that matters were proceeding in the regular
course. The day after Ingersoll and Du Ponceau had declined representing Tench
Coxe, Rawle wrote Ingersoll about the need for additional copies of the special
verdict because "there will be on the bench two Judges who did not hear the

former argument"; if Ingersoll produced one copy, Rawle would produce the other. The two justices hearing argument in the case for the first time would be Samuel Chase, restored to the bench after the impeachment proceeding, and Brockholst Livingston, a Jefferson appointment replacing Justice William Paterson, who had died.[8]

Only later that month did word leak out to John Redman Coxe that Tench Coxe did not intend to engage counsel to represent him in the Supreme Court hearing. "I called this morning," he wrote, "to express my regret, lest it might still further postpone the determination of the suit. I shall be obliged to you to inform me if this will be the effect—as my father's interest is so much at stake, that I wish to pursue it to the utmost, that no further delay may take place." Dr. Coxe had been prevented from seeing Tench Coxe because of the latter's reported indisposition, which may have been more than an issue of his physical well-being only.[9]

Tench Coxe tried to persuade his reluctant counsel that, having got what he regarded as inadequate notice from William Rawle of the scheduled reargument, the appellant was entitled to a postponement. At the last moment he achieved a tenuous rapprochement of some kind with Du Ponceau and Ingersoll; how tenuous may be gauged in the separate messages they sent Coxe as they were about to set off for Washington. Du Ponceau thought it his duty to disabuse Coxe of "your idea that you are entitled to a postponement for want of notice." Rawle had given "full notice" in time enough for Du Ponceau and Ingersoll to prepare for the Supreme Court hearing, which notice they in turn had communicated to Coxe—"and we cannot, if called upon, deny it." Du Ponceau regretted that he was leaving Philadelphia under a misunderstanding that ought to have been avoided. "A proper delicacy" kept him from saying more.[10]

Jared Ingersoll, true to form, didn't mince words: "The Cause of McIlvaine v. Cox will be postponed unless the Court order on the Argument in which case Mr. Duponceau & myself will make the best Defense we can; altho, you have neither paid us, nor promised us a Cent."[11]

None of this disagreement kept Coxe from volunteering further thinking on the need for a postponement. As the time drew near for Du Ponceau and Ingersoll to "make the best Defense we can," he sent them by expedited delivery a long letter explaining why it was advisable not to argue the case now and why the opposition was hastening to do so:

> The expectation that Chief Justice Marshall will sit, who is very particularly circumstanced, is one of their reasons for their urgency and from [sic] my

[8] Rawle to Ingersoll, Jan. 14, 1807, CFP, box 72, folder 13.
[9] J. R. Coxe to Tench Coxe, Jan. 24, 1807, CFP, box 72, folder 14.
[10] Du Ponceau to Coxe, Jan. 27, 1807, CFP, box 72, folder 14
[11] Ingersoll to Coxe, Jan. 28, 1807, CFP, ibid.

wishing to avoid so sudden a Turn. I do not believe they expect any thing in their favor from Judges C & L. It is two years since the argument—& now they press a new one, & accompany it with the information that Mr. Marshall is to sit. The settlement of this principle ought not to be precipitated—particularly against us. The alien getting an unfounded or hurried decision may sell & transfer the Money from the Country. The Citizen side cannot. . . . I think no attempt should be made by the other side to force on an argument for which I have not prepared not believing that I was obliged to meet the same expence over again at the pleasure or suggestion of the other side.[12]

Du Ponceau wrote from Washington on February 7 that he and Ingersoll "have according to your desire laid before the Court the whole State of facts respecting the Notice, notwithstanding which the Cause has been ordered on. It would have been heard today, but that Judge Cushing was not [in] Court, & he has expressed a wish to hear the reargument." The two lawyers had determined, he said, to act "without considering how we may be affected in point of professional emolument, & not to permit a Cause of this magnitude to suffer at this late moment for want of our best & most strenuous exertions." They were fully prepared: "we think the Cause good, & that the present time & the present Bench are as favorable as any that may hereafter obtain."

On February 9, Du Ponceau wrote Coxe that they expected the case to be argued the following day. However, Du Ponceau informed Coxe ten days later, "The cause of McIlvaine v. Coxe has been continued to next Term, on acct. of the indisposition of two of the Judges."[13]

When the case was firmly fixed on the Court's docket for the February 1808 term, the issue of legal fees remained a problem. Tench Coxe tried to raise money by tapping the interest he had in the estate of his deceased sister Mary. He applied to his brothers John and William Coxe, as executors of her estate, for an advance on account of the expected costs of engaging counsel, repeating that he had already paid $700 for the fees and expenses of counsel in the prior argument before the Supreme Court. He felt it "burdensome and unequal" to be out of pocket this sum while having to make the same outlay as Du Ponceau and Ingersoll were preparing to leave for Washington.[14]

Very late in the day an effort was made to settle the litigation. Tench Coxe, William Coxe, and Daniel W. Coxe jointly signed a letter addressed to Phineas Bond and Dr. John Redman Coxe to lay before them a settlement proposal. The

---

[12] Coxe to Ingersoll and Du Ponceau, Feb. 3, 1807 (retained copy), CFP, box 73, folder 1. By "Judges C & L" Coxe presumably meant Justices Chase and Livingston. As for the recurrent issue whether Marshall would sit or not, this letter serves as evidence tending to confirm that he had announced his withdrawal at the prior hearing in 1805, for his possible sitting now would seem to be regarded as a new development.

[13] Du Ponceau to Coxe, Feb. 7, 9, and 20, 1807, CFP, box 73, folder 1.

[14] TC to JDC and WC, Jr., Jan. 14, 1808 (retained copy), CFP, box 74, folder 4.

letter opened with a bit of wishful thinking—that "circumstances have arisen in the course of the last twelve months which augment the chances of a favourable issue to us of the litigated case of the Inheritance pending between our two families." The three brothers proposed "giving the two children of our Uncle Daniel Coxe and the seven children of our father, or their representatives, an equal participation in the Real estate of our aunt Rebecca Coxe." In other words, Daniel Coxe and his sister Grace Kempe would each get a one-ninth share as against a one-quarter share if they succeeded in the Supreme Court.

Why this offer to settle so late in the proceeding? Ostensibly because of the recent arrival in the United States of the wife of Daniel Coxe and the mother of John Redman Coxe, the brothers decided to take the initiative, subject, however, to the requirement that their offer be accepted within seven days. If not, "we shall consider Mrs. Coxe as preferring that the law should decide on our respective claims." Judge Coxe did not sign the letter, but his brothers wrote that they were "authorized to say that John D. Coxe makes no opposition to the proposition herein made."[15]

Whether the three Coxe brothers intended the settlement offer to be taken seriously is unclear. It is unclear, for example, that there were seven credible full participants on their side.[16] In reality, the settlement offer appeared prompted by Tench Coxe's urgent need for funds to cover expenses going forward. All four brothers met at Daniel W. Coxe's house to consider what should be done. Out of that meeting came the settlement proposal that William Coxe submitted to Tench Coxe, as having been read and revised by Judge John Coxe. Tench Coxe understood that, were the settlement offer thereafter rejected, his three brothers, including Judge Coxe, would pay their proportionate shares.

But no sooner was the settlement offer made than Judge Coxe wrote that he would "not contribute to the carrying on of the suit" and that "this may be considered as my final Determination." That message put Tench Coxe in an awkward bind as he had assured Messrs. Du Ponceau and Ingersoll, packing their bags to leave for Washington, that the four brothers would pay their fees.[17]

On the strength of that assurance Du Ponceau had written to Tench Coxe that he and Jared Ingersoll had been "assiduously employed these 10 days past, in

---

[15]TC, WC, and DWC, to Phineas Bond and Dr. John Redman Coxe, "Attornies of Danl Coxe and Mrs. Grace Kempe," Jan. 22, 1808 (a file copy), CFP, box 74, folder 5. Benjamin Rush visited Daniel Coxe's wife on September 20, 1807, and recorded that she had just arrived in Philadelphia, out of a concern for her aged parents, after an absence of more than twenty years. *Autobiography of Benjamin Rush*, ed. Corner, 272.

[16]In addition to the four Coxe brothers, the other candidate claimants through William Coxe, Sr., would have been the estate of his daughter Mary, who died, unmarried, in 1804; the children of his deceased daughter Sarah, who had married Andrew Allen; and Rebecca McIlvaine, the nominal party in the pending litigation, who was the only child of his deceased daughter, Rebecca McIlvaine, all of whose interests in Rebecca's Coxe estate might be deemed attenuated to one degree or another.

[17]John D. Coxe to Tench Coxe, Jan. 25, 1808, CFP, box 74, folder 5; TC to JDC, Jan. 26, 1808 (retained copy), CFP, ibid.

preparation for the argument. We have had several conferences, & are fully agreed as to the plan to be pursued & arguments to be used."[18] Two days later, just after Judge Coxe had delivered his surprise declaration, Du Ponceau notified Coxe that they were setting out early "on acct. of the badness of the roads" and that "[i]t will be well therefore that every thing preparatory to our journey be settled between us this afternoon." It wasn't settled, and in another message of that same date, Du Ponceau put the specific question about their prior understanding: "Do you mean that we are to receive $300 each before we leave town in the Cause of McIlvaine & Cox [sic] according to our proposal?"[19]

Coxe had no choice but to own up to the problem he had. The next day Ingersoll and Du Ponceau wrote that, "as the hour of their departure was drawing near," they wanted the matter fixed before they left and were willing, in lieu of cash in hand, to take "your Note at sixty days endorsed by any of your Brothers, or either of their Notes endorsed by you."[20] Some such expedient solution must have been found. The two lawyers left for Washington, and on the eve of the Supreme Court's hearing the case, Tench Coxe wrote his brother William Coxe that withdrawing at that stage was impossible—"it would carry a very unsatisfactory appearance"—especially after using the confident language they had in the settlement proposal.[21]

The case of *McIlvaine v. Coxe's Lessee* was argued for the second time on February 3, 4, and 5, 1808, before a bench consisting of Chief Justice Marshall and Associate Justices Cushing, Chase, Washington, and Livingston. The minutes show Justice Johnson as being absent, and the seventh member of an enlarged Court, newly appointed by Thomas Jefferson, Thomas Todd of Kentucky, did not take his seat until the following Monday, February 8. Of those sitting this time, Justices Chase and Livingston had not heard argument in 1805.

Judge Cranch prefaced his published report of the decision by stating that, in view of the space given to the arguments in 1805, he thought it unnecessary to provide other than a compressed summary of counsels' arguments on this occasion. From his summary, it does not appear that any new ground was broken, and yet the approach of each of the four lawyers addressing the court was far from perfunctory. Du Ponceau spoke first on Wednesday, February 3; he resumed his presentation the next day, when he was followed by William Rawle for Daniel Coxe and his sister; the concluding arguments at Friday's session were by Edward Tilghman in support of Rawle and by Jared Ingersoll for Tench Coxe. In keeping with its rapid decision-making process, the Court announced its decision on February 23:

---

[18] Du Ponceau to TC, [Jan. 24, 1808, as docketed], CFP, ibid.
[19] Du Ponceau to TC, Jan 26 and 26, 1808, CFP, ibid.
[20] Ingersoll and Du Ponceau to TC, Jan. 27, 1808. CFP, ibid.
[21] TC to WC Feb. 2, 1808 (retained copy), CFP, box 74, folder 6.

> This cause came to be heard on the Transcript of the Record of the Circuit Court of New Jersey and was argued by Counsel on consideration whereof it is adjudged and decreed that the Judgment of the Circuit Court be and the same is hereby affirmed with costs.[22]

On that same day, a lawyer of already recognized talent in the profession, though not yet thirty, was formally admitted to practice before the Supreme Court. Joseph Story of Massachusetts had arrived a few days earlier in what he termed "the wilderness of Washington" and found that "[t]he scene of my greatest amusement, as well as instruction, is the Supreme Court," where "I daily spend several hours . . . and generally, when disengaged, dine and sup with the judges." Three years later, on President Madison's nomination, he would join the Supreme Court as its youngest member.

Story had not arrived in Washington in time to hear the arguments in *McIlvaine v. Coxe's Lessee*, but he did hear at least the tail end of nine days of argument in two companion cases that the Court treated as one and in which the lawyers in *McIlvaine* argued but this time in a different alignment: Rawle and Ingersoll were on one side, and Du Ponceau and Edward Tilghman on the other.[23] In a letter to a friend back home, Story had something to say about each of them. It will suffice here to give his appraisals of the two lawyers who had argued for Tench Coxe.

Du Ponceau was, he observed, a Frenchman by birth, "a very ingenious counsellor," having "the reputation for great subtilty and acuteness," and "excessively minute in the display of his learning." Nor did Story stop there in this less-than-flattering portrait of Du Ponceau:

> His manner is animated but not impressive, and he betrays at every turn the impatience and casuistry of his nation. His countenance is striking, his figure rather awkward. A small, sparkling, black eye, and a thin face, satisfy you that he is not without quickness of mind; yet he seemed to me to exhaust himself in petty distinctions, and in a perpetual recurrence to doubtful, if not to inconclusive arguments. His reasoning was rather sprightly and plausible, than logical and coercive; in short, he is a French advocate.

Of Jared Ingersoll, he was no more sparing in portraiture: "rather a peculiar face, and yet in person or manner has nothing which interests in a high degree. He is more animated than Rawle, but has less precision; he is learned, laborious,

---

[22] Minutes of the Supreme Court, Feb. 3, 4, 5, and 23, 1808. *McIlvaine v. Coxe's Lessee*, 8 U.S. (4 Cranch) 209 (1808), is accessible online at: https://supreme.justia.com/cases/federal/us/8/209/case.html.

[23] The companion cases that Story heard argued were *Rose v. Himely*, 8 U.S. (4 Cranch) 241, and *Hudson v. Guestier*, 8 U.S. (4 Cranch) 293 (1808).

and minute, not eloquent, not declamatory, but diffuse. The Pennsylvanians consider him a perfect drag-net, that gathers every thing in its course."[24]

It would appear that counsel for the parties heard little other than the announcement of the result on February 23. Peter Du Ponceau sent this letter to Tench Coxe after he returned to Philadelphia:

> I have not got any more than yourself the particulars respecting the decision in the case of McIlvaine v. Coxe. I am told that Mr. E. Tilghman has received a letter from Judge Cranch, in which he tells him that the Cause has been decided in favor of Dr. Coxe by five Judges against one, & that the division was entirely on the ground of the New Jersey Act. I have not seen the Letter, but I do not doubt that you may have communication of it from Mr. Tilghman.
>
> If Mr. Danl Coxe has been adjudged to be a Citizen of N. Jersey, I am afraid that it decides the question as to lands in other States by virtue of the 2d § of the 4th Art of the Constitution of the U.S.[25]

We confront a puzzle in this communication from Du Ponceau. In his report of the decision, Judge Cranch records that "Johnson, J. did not vote upon the question, and Todd, J. gave no opinion, as he had not been present at the argument."[26] Johnson's failure to vote is unexplained; he was present at the argument in 1805; the Supreme Court minutes show him absent during the argument in 1808, but he returned to the bench in the cases that immediately followed. With these two justices abstaining, the Court was reduced to four members (Cushing, Chase, Washington, and Livingston), that is, assuming that Chief Justice Marshall had disqualified himself as he reportedly did in 1805. Yet Du Ponceau has the Court dividing five to one. Unless he had a shaky

---

[24] Story [adopting a nom de plume of "Matthew Bramble"] to Samuel P. P. Fay, Washington, Feb. 16, 1808, in *Life and Letters of Joseph Story*, ed. William W. Story, 2 vols. (London: John Chapman, 1851), 1:162–63. In a subsequent letter to the same friend, Story provided his impressions of members of the Supreme Court whose colleague he would soon become. Peter S. Du Ponceau, in full perspective, merits a more appreciative assessment. He was not only an accomplished lawyer, who showed exemplary patience in dealing with Tench Coxe as his client, but also a pioneer in ethnographic and linguistic studies of the American Indian; he became the president of the American Philosophical Society in 1827, serving in that position until his death in 1844.

[25] Du Ponceau to Coxe, Feb. 8, 1808 [mistaken date, Feb. 28?], CFP, box 74, folder 6. Article 4, Section 2 of the Constitution reads in relevant part: "The citizens of each State shall be entitled to all the privileges and immunities of citizens in the several States."

[26] *McIlvaine v. Coxe's Lessee*, 8 U.S. (4 Cranch) 209, 211 (1808).

perception of who was sitting when that case was argued, the numbers don't add up.[27]

Du Ponceau may conceivably have confused the membership of the Court in *McIlvaine* with the one consisting of six justices that sat in *Rose v. Himely*,[28] in which he appeared as counsel and that wound up dividing five to one in a decision announced on March 2, 1808 (Justice Johnson dissenting). In his report to Coxe, it is also possible that Du Ponceau remained shaken by an accident that occurred on the way back from Washington. The driver of the carriage transporting the former adversaries in *McIlvaine*, distracted by his passengers' raucous recollection of the witticisms they had inflicted on each other in arguing that case, missed seeing a tree stump in the road. On impact he was thrown from his seat, leaving the lawyers to bail out unceremoniously from the runaway carriage. As Du Ponceau recalled the incident with amusement thirty years later, a surgeon was summoned in Baltimore to attend to his injured companions, all of whom he bled—Du Ponceau alone declining that service.[29]

In March, Tench Coxe wrote his brother William that he was waiting for "a copy of the Judges speeches or explanatory observations in giving the Judgmt in the case of McIlvaine & Coxe." Despite Du Ponceau's advice that the litigation was conclusively over, Coxe felt that "we have a right to see the act that decides so large a property." It took two more months before he received a manuscript copy from Washington of the Court's unsigned opinion. Only in Cranch's published report is the authorship finally credited to the senior member of the Court, Justice William Cushing (Figure 4).[30]

For all of the Herculean labors of counsel in 1805 and 1808 and their citing authorities hither and yon, Justice Cushing's opinion is a tightly reasoned one, devoid of any reference to prior cases or commentary. Herbert Johnson, in the volume for that period of the Holmes Devise, has described the opinion as "lengthy and erudite," which he deemed "well beyond [Cushing's] capacities at

---

[27] Perhaps one should pause before assuming that Marshall scrupulously abstained in 1808 even though the terms of the recusal that Judge Cranch ascribed to him in 1805 ("The Chief Justice did not sit in this cause, having formed a decided opinion on the principal question. . . . ") would have made it difficult to conclude three years later, after Cranch's report of the 1805 proceeding had been published, that he might reverse course and participate in the Court's decision. Yet in reporting the decision of 1808 and footnoting the nonparticipation of Justices Johnson and Todd, Cranch omitted in his head count any mention of the Chief Justice.

[28] 8 U.S. (4 Cranch) 241. Judge Cranch reported that the newly appointed Justice Todd did not sit in this case (ibid. at 242); otherwise the bench was at its fully enlarged strength.

[29] Letter of Du Ponceau to Wharton, June 3, 1837, as an appendix to Wharton's memorial essay for William Rawle, in *Memoirs of the Historical Society of Pennsylvania*, vol. 4. pt. 1, 86–88. Of the condition of the roads of that era, Joseph Story wrote: "Between Philadelphia and Baltimore, one hundred miles, and between Baltimore and Washington, forty miles, are as execrable roads as can be found in Christendom." Story to Samuel P. P. Fay, Washington, May 23, 1807, in *Life and Letters of Joseph Story*, 1:148.

[30] TC to WC, March 25, 1808 (retained copy), CFP, box 74, folder 9. The manuscript opinion of five pages headed "McIlviane v. Cox [sic]" is found in CFP, box 74, folder 12, and docketed "McIlvaine v. Cox [sic], opinion of the court, $1.25 Paid by Tench Coxe, May 9, 1808."

Figure 4. Portrait of Justice William Cushing, pastel on paper, circa 1796–97, attributed to James Sharples and showing Cushing wearing an English-style wig, one of the last American judges to do so.

Courtesy of Independence National Historical Park, Philadelphia.

that time and perhaps beyond his professional ability even at a younger age."
One may quibble about how lengthy and erudite the opinion was, but Professor
Johnson has raised a question that he leaves suggestively unanswered: If Cushing
didn't author it, who did?[31]

Following the approach taken in his concurring opinion in *Talbot v. Jansen*
and by Chief Justice Marshall in *The Charming Betsy*, Justice Cushing, as the
nominal author of the opinion in McIlvaine, was careful to say what the Court
was not deciding. It found it "unnecessary to declare an opinion upon a point
which has been much debated in this cause, whether a real British subject born
before the 4th of July, 1776; who never from the time of his birth, resided within
any of the American colonies or states, can, upon the principles of the common
law, take lands by descent in the United States." Daniel Coxe was not that
person, having been born and resided in New Jersey long before the Declaration
of Independence.[32]

Nor did the Court need to decide when precisely "Daniel Coxe lost his right
of election to abandon the American cause, and to adhere to his allegiance to
the king of Great Britain," because it accepted the argument his counsel made
on his behalf that, by remaining in New Jersey after that state had adopted its
new constitution and, more particularly, after it had passed the act of October
4, 1776, he became a citizen of New Jersey by tacit assent.[33]

The third disclaimer related to the right of expatriation. The Court expressed
no opinion as to its possible existence under the common law, or "upon the
application of that principle to a person born in the state of New Jersey, before
its separation from the mother country." It again accepted the analysis of counsel
for Daniel Coxe in holding that New Jersey, through subsequent legislative action,
had "asserted its right to the allegiance of such of its citizens as had left the
state, and had not attempted to return to their former allegiance," referring to
them as "fugitives" and not as "aliens." Similarly, when the New Jersey legislature
provided that Coxe lose his property for having joined the British army, it was
not for the purpose of condemning him personally, "which would have been most
unjust," but only to assess a penalty by way of confiscation.[34]

Going beyond the record strictly before it, the Court summarized its holding
thus far:

---

[31] Holmes Devise, vol. 2, Haskins and Johnson, *History of the Supreme Court of the United States*, 384.

[32] *McIlvaine v. Coxe's Lessee*, 8 U.S. (4 Cranch) at 211.

[33] 8 U.S. (4 Cranch) at 211–12.

[34] 8 U.S. (4 Cranch) at 212–14. It may be reasonably questioned whether New Jersey so decisively drew
the distinctions the Court attributed to it. Would New Jersey have regarded proceeding by attainder as "most
unjust"? Governor Livingston of New Jersey was outspoken in urging the harshest treatment of those collaborating
with the British. Pennsylvania and other states had recourse to attainder and outlawry proceedings directed
against Tories. See Bradley Chapin, *The American Law of Treason: Revolutionary and Early National Origins*
(Seattle: University of Washington Press, 1964), 48–50, 75–80. In apparent opposition to Justice Cushing's
volunteered remark, the Supreme Court had previously declined to invalidate a Georgia attainder statute in
Cooper v. Telfair, 4 U.S. (4 Dall.) 14 (1800).

Having taken this view of the laws of New-Jersey upon this subject, it may be safely asserted that prior to the treaty of peace, it would not have been competent, even for the state to allege alienage in Daniel Coxe in the face of repeated declarations of the legitimate authority of the government, that he continued to owe allegiance to the state, notwithstanding all his attempts to throw it off. If he was an alien, he must have been so by the laws of New-Jersey; but those laws had uniformly asserted, that he was an offender against the form of his allegiance to the state. How then can this court, acting upon the laws of New-Jersey declare him an alien? The conclusion is inevitable, that, prior to the treaty of peace, Daniel Coxe was entitled to hold, and had a capacity to take lands in New-Jersey by descent.[35]

That left only the hurdle of the treaty of peace to get over. The Court was persuaded that nothing in that instrument altered Daniel Coxe's status or conferred on him what he lacked before, which was the right to cast off his allegiance to New Jersey in acknowledgment of his allegiance to the British king: "It left all persons in the situation it found them, neither making those citizens, who had by the laws of the states been declared aliens, nor releasing from their allegiance, any who had become, and were claimed as citizens." If, during the period leading up to the treaty of peace, the laws of New Jersey about citizenship were to be regarded, "in the language of one of the counsel [for Tench Coxe], temporary and *functi officio*, they were certainly not rendered so by the treaty of peace, nor by the political situation of the two nations, in consequence of it." For the Court to accept that contention would be not only to disregard state sovereignty, "anterior to, and independent of the treaty," but to adopt a doctrine that "might be productive of more mischief than it is possible for us to foresee."[36]

Accordingly, the judgment below was affirmed with costs. After two exhaustive submissions to the Supreme Court, one may ask whether the Court had any choice but to rule as it did for Daniel Coxe. The revolutionary imperative denied the disaffected virtually any safe opportunity to confirm their loyalty to the king while remaining in this country. They had no real alternative but to leave, and to leave quickly, before their continuing residence, their "abiding," was taken as irrevocable proof of their assenting to their new citizenship. Such was the lesson of the frequently cited Pennsylvania precedent of *Respublica v. Chapman*, in which Thomas McKean extricated Samuel Chapman from a charge of treason because Chapman left the Commonwealth and joined the British army before the expiration of a statutory grace period, running in McKean's calculation from July

---

[35] 8 U.S. (4 Cranch) at 214.

[36] 8 U.S. (4 Cranch) at 214–15. *Functi officio*: [the laws] expired having fulfilled their purpose. One risk of adopting such a doctrine might be to call into question, after years had passed, transfers of title made to third parties under various confiscatory schemes that states adopted during the Revolution and enforced against those thought to have sided with the British. Kettner, *American Citizenship*, 180, 202–209.

4, 1776, to February 11, 1777. The court in *McIlvaine* followed much the same reasoning in conferring citizenship on Daniel Coxe as a consequence of his being present in New Jersey during a considerably shorter period, from July 4 to October 4, 1776. The irony is that what Daniel Coxe might have thought a burden in 1776 became a benefit for him in 1808.

The Court could not, of course, ignore the overwhelming evidence that Daniel Coxe had from an early date in the Revolution consistently identified himself as a British subject, to the exclusion of any other call on his allegiance, at least until his aunt's death in 1802 revived a newfound attachment to the country of his birth. The convincing weight of that evidence may have accounted for the Court's inability to reach a decision in 1805. Elsewhere, as we have seen, it carefully avoided passing on an individual's right of expatriation, but in this case, the Court came close to affirming, without saying so, the doctrine of perpetual allegiance as applicable to the new citizenship that independence conferred on the willing and unwilling alike. To have held otherwise, by recognizing a unilateral right of expatriation, would have represented a major departure, unsupported by precedent and having the potential to undermine aspects of the Revolution's settlement that were still open to debate.

Immediately after its decision in *McIlvaine*, the Supreme Court moved to dispose of a question it left open in *McIlvaine* concerning the *antenati*. Russell Lee, a citizen of the United States, died in 1793; lands he owned would have passed by inheritance to Mrs. Dawson unless her status as an alien barred her from taking them. Mrs. Dawson was born in England before the year 1775, always remained a British subject, and never came to the United States. It was maintained on her behalf that a community of allegiance existed at her birth entitling her to inherit in the same way that an American citizen then born might inherit land in England. Justice Johnson made short work of that proposition, holding that the frame of reference was not the time of birth but the time of Russell Lee's death, of "descent cast," when Mrs. Dawson was clearly a foreigner, never having owed allegiance to an American state or government. Anything to the contrary emanating from *Calvin's Case*, Justice Johnson dismissed as mere dictum.[37]

The decision in *McIlvaine v. Coxe's Lessee* didn't mark the end of Coxe family claims; nor, to paraphrase Justice Cushing, did it reduce the risk of mischief-making for judges before whom the Revolution would continue to be fought.

---

[37] *Dawson's Lessee v. Godfrey*, 8 U.S. (4 Cranch) 321 (1808). A similar case came before the Pennsylvania Supreme Court, and, in reaching the same result, Chief Justice William Tilghman said that it would have been more agreeable to him if he could have avoided expressing an opinion on the matter because of the risk he felt that, "having argued the same point at the bar of the Supreme Court in the case of M'Ilvaine v. Coxe, . . . my mind may have retained some of the impression it received in preparing for the argument." *Lessee of Jackson v. Burns*, 3 Binn. 75, 86–87 (Pa. Sup. Ct. 1810).

7

Afterward

Grace Coxe Kempe, Daniel Coxe's sister, attempted to recover property in New Jersey that she had owned in her own name before her marriage to John Tabor Kempe and that the state confiscated as punishment for his alleged treason. The suit she brought made its way to the Supreme Court in a decision handed down a year after *McIlvaine*. Chief Justice Marshall spoke for the court in an opinion reminiscent of his famous opinion in *Marbury v. Madison* (1803) inasmuch as he found that Mrs. Kempe had been improperly deprived of her property but that the Court lacked jurisdiction to grant her relief.[1]

In its decision in *McIlvaine*, the Supreme Court awarded recovery of court costs to Daniel Coxe and his sister as the prevailing parties. The certified total for both the Circuit Court and the Supreme Court came to £20.14.4, or $56.58. Thomas Cadwalader, acting on behalf of his client Mrs. Kempe, inquired of Richard Stockton whether any person on the losing side could be held responsible for paying this sum.

It was a hopeless task, Stockton replied. The only party of record was Rebecca McIlvaine, now married and the wife of Joshua Maddox Wallace, against whom Stockton thought bringing an action to recover costs would yield nothing. He underscored the staged character of the proceeding from the outset: "I even doubt whether Mrs. Wallace would be at all answerable—it was an amicable Suit, conducted under an agreement between Mr. Bond and Tench Coxe. Miss McIlvaine was probably never consulted, and perhaps never assented to her name being used."[2]

Dr. John Redman Coxe spent the next twenty-five years trying to achieve a settlement with the children of Grace Kempe concerning the more substantial expenses incurred in the successful litigation. When the parties eventually got down to specific items, Mrs. Kempe's son in England, Edward Kempe, was unable to reconcile two separate accountings prepared and submitted to his mother: one by Phineas Bond and another by John Redman Coxe. His sense of family propriety stopped him just short of charging that his mother was being double-billed her share of the expenses. In 1833, Dr. Coxe betrayed fatigue and frustration when he wrote to Thomas Cadwalader: "Will you permit me to remind you of our intended settlement relating to Mr. Kempe. As I shall probably be from home after about the middle of May, for an uncertain period, I should much desire to terminate this long standing account."[3]

Daniel Coxe died in England in 1826. His widow, Sarah Redman Coxe, brought suit in New Jersey demanding as her dower right a third part of certain lands

---

[1] *Kempe's Lessee v. Kennedy*, 9 U.S. (5 Cranch) 173 (1809).

[2] The bill of costs, n.d., is in CadP, box 136, folder 6; Stockton to Cadwalader, Dec. 20, 1809, CadP, box 157, folder 5. The present purchasing power of the 1809 cost total would come to $1,130 (http://www.measuring worth.com/).

[3] Edward Kempe to Thomas Cadwalader, Sept. 23, 1818, enclosing a transcribed copy of the debtor's side of the Bond accounting, CadP, box 136, folder 5; Coxe to Cadwalader, Apr. 22, 1833, ibid.

that Daniel Coxe had owned. She succeeded in her claims—half a century after she and her husband had left New Jersey and title to the property that the state took through confiscation had passed to bona fide purchasers. As in *McIlvaine v. Coxe's Lessee*, her husband's alien status was asserted as a defense against her dower claim, provoking this outburst of indignation from a member of the New Jersey Supreme Court:

> He was on the 3d of July 1776, a subject of the king of Great-Britain; so was Hancock and Adams; so was General Washington and the band of patriots that composed his army, and must we gainsay their citizenship and declare them *aliens* to their country? Again, Daniel Coxe, in the year 1777, withdrew from this state; so did also a great many other Americans take refuge with the British army and were called refugees; but they were declared by all our statutes to *owe* allegiance to the state; they were declared to be citizens; were warned of their duties as citizens; and punished in their property as citizens; and we cannot call them aliens even at this day without flying in the face of all our laws. . . . The plea says, that he elected to continue and remain a subject of the king. Now, our laws do not permit a man to lay aside his allegiance as he puts off a garment, otherwise he might appear in arms against his country without being guilty of treason.[4]

In this period, the Supreme Court of the United States, and particularly Joseph Story (Figure 5), would struggle repeatedly with the issue of expatriation. Justice Story avoided ruling on the existence of the right of expatriation in another complicated prize case, *The Santissima Trinidad*, which came before the Court in 1822, although he appeared to be leaning in the direction of recognizing such a right: "Assuming for the purposes of argument that an American citizen may, independently of any legislative act to this effect, throw off his allegiance to his native country, as to which we give no opinion, it is perfectly clear that this cannot be done without a *bona fide* change of domicile under circumstances of good faith." Story anticipated that the time might come when the doctrine would "become the leading point of a judgment of the Court."[5]

For Justice Story, if not for the Court as a whole, the moment for reassessing the holding in *McIlvaine v. Coxe's Lessee* came in two 1830 cases. The first case, *Inglis v. Trustees of Sailor's Snug Harbor*, called into question the validity of a charitable gift that Captain Robert Richard Randall had made under elaborately drafted provisions in his will to establish a retirement community for "aged, decrepit and worn out seamen." John Inglis, an Anglican bishop, contested the

---

[4] *Coxe v. Gulick*, 10 N.J.L. (5 Halst.) 328, 330–31 (1829); see also *Coxe v. Higbee*, 11 N.J.L. (6 Halst.) 395 (1830), and E. Alfred Jones, *The Loyalists of New Jersey: Their Memorials, Petitions, Claims. Etc. From English Records* (Newark, NJ: New Jersey Historical Society, 1921), 54. Sarah Redman Coxe died in Brighton, England, in 1843, at age ninety-one.

[5] *The Santissima Trinidad*, 20 U.S. (7 Wheat.) 283, 347–48 (1822).

Figure 5. Daguerreotype of Justice Joseph Story by Mathew B. Brady, circa 1844, at about the time of Story's election to membership in the American Philosophical Society and near the end of his life.

Courtesy of the Library of Congress, LC-USZ62-110196.

validity of the will; if successful in that challenge, he would have taken by inheritance Randall's estate as his nearest, albeit a distant, relative.[6]

The majority of the Supreme Court upheld the provisions in the will, which might have ended its inquiry; nevertheless, Justice Thompson, acting for the majority, went on to examine, among other questions certified on appeal, the possible inability of John Inglis to inherit because of his alienage. Inglis was born in New York at an unascertained time after the Declaration of Independence. His mother died on the eve of the British evacuation of the city in 1783; he and his father, a dedicated and articulate loyalist, left for England in November of that year, where they remained until 1787 when his father was consecrated the Anglican Bishop of Nova Scotia. Of no more than five years of age when he left New York, John Inglis later followed his father by entering the clergy and succeeding him as Bishop of Nova Scotia, the position he held at the time of this proceeding.[7]

Although not necessary to sustain its holding on the provisions in the will, the majority opinion found that, as a consequence of leaving New York and staying abroad, the second Bishop Inglis had surrendered any vestige of American citizenship he might have acquired either by birth or by residing with his parents in this country.[8] For Justice Story, who was unable, in dissent, to accept the validity of the dispositive provisions in the will,[9] it became more than an academic exercise to ascertain whether Bishop Inglis had retained his citizenship under New York law. Although he concurred with the majority in its finding that he lost that citizenship, if he ever had it, Story introduced greater clarity in the analysis of how citizenship might be acquired and lost during the Revolution than the Supreme Court had succeeded in doing at any time in the past.

Justice Story reviewed the common-law principles that fixed one's allegiance at birth, an allegiance that thereafter could not be dissolved except with the consent of the sovereign or by conquest or abdication of the sovereign. He termed "a case of more nicety and intricacy . . . when a country is divided by civil war and each party establishes a separate and independent form of government." Moreover, he regarded as a case apart—"*sui generis*" was his term—the separation of the United States from Great Britain, "treated on many occasions, both at the bar and on the bench," since the Declaration of Independence and the Revolution

---

[6] *Inglis v. Trustees of Sailor's Snug Harbor*, 28 U.S. (3 Pet.) 99 (1830). The organization's correct name has "Sailor" plural, not singular, as in the case report. According to legend, the artfully drawn provisions in Captain Randall's will were the handiwork of Alexander Hamilton. For background generally about Sailors' Snug Harbor and Hamilton's supposed role as scrivener, see Gerald J. Barry, *The Sailors' Snug Harbor: A History* (New York: Fordham University Press, 2000).

[7] Charles Inglis, the father, was no passive man of the cloth. He mounted a polemical attack against Thomas Paine and, as rector of Trinity Church in New York during the British occupation of that city, constantly preached indissoluble fidelity to the king. See Jasanoff, *Liberty's Exiles*, 29–31, 147–50.

[8] 28 U.S. (3 Pet.) at 119–27.

[9] 28 U.S. (3 Pet.) at 154.

did not effect an entire dissolution of the government of the former colonies. In that particular situation, the common law provided no sure guide. "If . . . it was said that all persons born within a colony owed a perpetual allegiance to that colony, whoever might be the sovereign, the answer was that the common law admitted no right in any part of the subjects to change their allegiance without the consent of their sovereign, and the usurpation of such authority was itself rebellion, for *'nemo potest exuere patriam'* was the language of the common law." In the peculiar circumstances of the Revolution, Story ventured the view that "the general—I will not say the universal—principle was to consider all persons, whether natives or inhabitants, upon the occurrence of the Revolution, entitled to make their choice either to remain subjects of the British Crown, or to become members of the United States."

So far, so good, one might agree, at least in theory. In facing the more vexing question of when the choice had to be made, Story took refuge in a familiar escape formula used by lawyers and judges: "within a reasonable time." To be sure, it was something of a stretch for him to accept as reasonable the short time intervals Pennsylvania and New Jersey granted dissenters before lingering in those states bound them to citizenship, as determined in *Respublica v. Chapman* and *McIlvaine v. Coxe's Lessee*, to which Story referred.[10]

The critical point of departure for Story came in the next question he posed for an answer—whether any person, having thus acquired citizenship by operation of law, could divest himself of it—and here he parted company with Justice Cushing's opinion in *McIlvaine v. Coxe's Lessee*. He thought that the treaty of peace in 1783 was the pivotal moment when the issue of allegiance could be resolved and when those who adhered to the king might be discharged from any opposing claim of allegiance and sovereignty. In coming to this conclusion, he was forced to admit that the language in the Court's decision in *McIlvaine* weighed against him. For Story, however, it was "extremely difficult" to believe that the treaty did not require the interpretation that "each government should be finally deemed entitled to the allegiance of those who were at the time adhering to it."[11]

Had he been a member of the Supreme Court in 1808, rather than an observer present at its proceedings, would Justice Story have decided that Daniel Coxe had effectively cast off his American allegiance? The rationale he developed in this case of reciprocally discharged allegiances under the treaty of peace suggests a finding on his part that in 1783, if not before, Daniel Coxe had shed his temporary New Jersey citizenship and become a British subject.

That impression is strengthened in the second case in the 1830 term, *Shanks v. Dupont*,[12] the last jurisprudential effort by the Supreme Court to cope with

---

[10] 28 U.S. (3 Pet.) at 155–60.
[11] 28 U.S. (3 Pet.) at 161–71.
[12] 28 U.S. (3 Pet.) 242 (1830).

competing allegiances during the American Revolution. Justice Story, writing for the Court, applied the logic of his opinion in *Inglis* to arrive at what might strike some as a strained result.

The Court once again had before it a family inheritance controversy between the descendants of two sisters, each of them born in South Carolina before the Revolution. Their father, Thomas Scott, a native of South Carolina, died without a will in 1782, owning the land in dispute. Sarah, the mother of one set of descendants, remained in South Carolina all her life; it was conceded that her children had an uncontested right to one half of her father's landed estate. Ann, the other sister, who was also born before the Revolution, married a British officer in 1781 when Charleston was under the control of the British; upon the evacuation of Charleston in December 1782, she left with her husband for England where she remained until her death in 1801, having given birth there to five children, the claimants in this litigation to the other half of her father's estate.

Ann's children based their claim on a provision in the Jay treaty of 1794 that assured British subjects holding lands in the territories of the United States that they would continue "to hold them according to the nature and tenure of their respective estates and titles therein." They took an appeal to the Supreme Court from a decision of the South Carolina's highest court, which had held that Ann's children could not avail themselves of the protection of the treaty because their mother was an American citizen.[13]

In his opinion for the Court, Justice Story performed a delicate balancing act. As a preliminary matter, he established that Ann Scott remained a citizen of South Carolina even though the British had seized control of the state and exacted the allegiance of its conquered inhabitants. "[B]ut it was," he held, "a temporary allegiance which did not destroy but only suspend their former allegiance. It did not annihilate their allegiance to the State of South Carolina and make them *de facto* aliens." Nor did Ann Scott's marriage in 1781 to Joseph Shanks, a British officer, automatically work a change in her status, "because marriage with an alien, whether a friend or an enemy, produces no dissolution of the native allegiance of the wife."[14]

Upon descent cast in her father's estate, or more simply put, upon his death in 1782, Story reasoned that Ann Scott Shanks was not then barred by alienage from acquiring a vested one-half interest in her father's landed property. "The question, then," wrote Story, "is whether her subsequent removal with her husband

---

[13] 28 U.S. (3 Pet.) at 243–45.

[14] 28 U.S. (3 Pet.) at 245–46. Under Section 3 of the Expatriation Act of 1907, Congress provided that "any American woman who marries a foreigner shall take the nationality of her husband" and automatically lose her American citizenship for the duration of that marriage. Ch. 2534, 34 Stat. 1228–29 (1907). This statutory deprivation of citizenship was upheld by the Supreme Court in *Mackensie v. Hare*, 239 U.S. 299 (1915), but not without the Court's taking into momentary consideration (239 U.S. at 309) the contrary view that Justice Story had expressed in *Shanks v. Dupont*.

operated as a virtual dissolution of her allegiance and fixed her future allegiance to the British Crown by the Treaty of Peace of 1783." Story answered that question in the affirmative, finding her a British subject by choice and thus entitled to the protection of the 1794 treaty provisions, all of which in turn allowed her foreign-born children to succeed to her one-half share in her father's estate.[15]

John Marshall was notably silent in these two cases, although he had authorized Story to say that he agreed with him in *Inglis* as to the portion of Story's opinion holding the charitable devise invalid as written. There is reason to believe that the Chief Justice may have continued to subscribe to the doctrine of perpetual allegiance.[16] He and Justice William Johnson were the only members of this Court who were also members of the Court when *McIlvaine v. Coxe's Lessee* was decided, but with neither of them recorded as participating in that decision.[17] It is of more than passing interest, therefore, that in *Shanks v. Dupont* Justice Johnson dissented at length, stating that, although at one time he had been inclined to recognize a right of election to alter one's allegiance, upon more mature reflection he realized he was giving "too much weight to natural law and the suggestions of reason and justice."[18] He contended that the doctrine of perpetual allegiance was firmly grounded in precedent and principle and that "Mrs. Shanks continued, as she was born, a citizen of South Carolina, and of course unprotected by the British treaty."[19]

Justice Johnson sat as a member of the Court in 1805 for the extensive arguments of counsel in *McIlvaine v. Coxe's Lessee*. Although he was not present during the reargument in 1808 and abstained from voting on the outcome, he had clearly in mind the evidence of Daniel Coxe's adherence to the British cause and the effect Justice Story's analysis would have had if applied to Coxe's claim in the earlier case. Given that perspective, he could not resist one final thrust in his dissent: "it does appear to me, that in the case of *Coxe vs. M'Ilvaine* [*sic*], this court decided against the right of election most expressly; for if ever the exercise of will or choice might be inferred from the evidence, it is hardly possible for a stronger case to be made than that which is presented in the facts of that case."[20]

---

[15] 28 U.S. (3 Pet.) at 246–50.

[16] 28 U.S. (3 Pet.) at 154. See Holmes Devise, vols. 3–4, G. Edward White, *History of the Supreme Court of the United States: The Marshall Court and Cultural Change, 1815–35* (New York: Macmillan, 1988), 903 and n92. In *Inglis*, Marshall did, however, speak for the Court in denying an application for reargument submitted by Daniel Webster, as counsel for Bishop Inglis. 28 U.S. (3 Pet.) at 191–92.

[17] Justice Bushrod Washington was one of the four justices who participated in the *McIlvaine* decision; although he would have heard argument in both *Inglis* and *Shanks* during the February term of 1829, he died while sitting on circuit in Philadelphia in November of that year before the decisions were announced in these latter two cases. For the 1829 dates of argument, see http://www.supremecourt.gov/opinions/dates ofdecisions.pdf.

[18] 28 U.S. (3 Pet.) at 258.

[19] 28 U.S. (3 Pet.) at 265.

[20] Ibid.

APPENDIX

Members of the
American Philosophical Society
Mentioned in the Text or Footnotes
(with Dates of Election)

John Adams (1780)

Andrew Allen (1768)

Horace Binney (1808)

Thomas Cadwalader (1825)

Benjamin Chew (1768)

Daniel Coxe (1772)

John Redman Coxe (1799)

Tench Coxe (1796)

Peter S. Du Ponceau (1791)

Benjamin Franklin (1744)

William Franklin (1768)

Joseph Galloway (1768)

Alexander Hamilton (1780)

Jared Ingersoll (1781)

Thomas Jefferson (1780)

William Johnson (1810)

Edward Livingston (1825)

James Madison (1785)

John Marshall (1830)

Thomas McKean (1768)

Thomas Paine (1785)

William Rawle (1786)

John Redman (1768)

Benjamin Rush (1768)

Edward Shippen, Jr. (1768)

Samuel Shoemaker (1769)

Joseph Story (1844)

William Tilghman (1805)

Bushrod Washington (1805)

Daniel Webster (1837)

Thomas Willing (1768)

James Wilson (1768)

Glossary

alienage, disability of: As a general matter of common law, a person not born within the realm of the king of England was an alien and unable, subject to some engrafted exceptions, to hold title to real estate in England. That disability applied with particular force to prevent an alien from inheriting land through intestate descent. Not all of the former colonies recognized that bar to inheritance, but the state of New Jersey did.

antenatus (*antenati*), *postnatus* (*postnati*): Reference points derived from *Calvin's Case* (1608) where it was held that one born in Scotland after (*postnatus*) the accession of James VI of Scotland to the throne of England as James I could take title to real estate located in England, but not one born before (*antenatus*). The terms were subsequently used to designate persons born before the Declaration of Independence and after it, whether in America or in England.

attainder, attainted: Action taken by the legislature (a bill of attainder) or, less typically, by the executive body in declaring a named individual or individuals guilty of treason or another major felony, resulting in the forfeiture of the condemned person's property and civil rights. Daniel Coxe and Tench Coxe were named under a proclamation of conditional attainder issued by the Pennsylvania Supreme Executive Council, requiring them to surrender for trial by a specified date, or failing to do so, suffer the punishment of being attainted. Sections 9 and 10 of Article 1 of the United States Constitution contain provisions specifically directed against this practice by prohibiting Congress and any state from passing a bill of attainder.

descent cast: The devolving of real estate upon the death of the owner dying intestate, that is, without a will, the date of death fixing the time for ascertaining a claimant's citizenship.

diversity of citizenship, diversity jurisdiction: Section 2 of Article 3 of the United States Constitution extends the judicial power of federal courts to controversies "between Citizens of different States . . . and between the citizens [of a State] . . . and the Citizens or Subjects [of foreign States]." Establishing diversity of citizenship and obtaining eventual access to the Supreme Court became a preoccupation of counsel for the parties in *McIlvaine v. Coxe's Lessee*.

ejectment, action of: Originally conceived at common law as an action for possession of a leasehold interest, it was converted through the ingenuity of common lawyers into an action to adjudicate title to real estate, in which the real parties in interest were disguised under fictitious names and the issue was joined by the allegation of a forcible ejectment that existed as a circumstance only in the pleadings.

expatriation: Whether one had the unilateral right to renounce one's birthright allegiance was a question much mooted in the arguments of counsel before the Supreme Court in *McIlvaine v. Coxe's Lessee*. The **doctrine of perpetual allegiance**—*nemo potest exuere patriam*, no one can renounce his country—found grounding in *Calvin's Case*. Were **expatriation** and **emigration** equivalent rights as some state constitutions of the revolutionary period might be taken as recognizing? In the continuing absence of an authoritative ruling by the Supreme Court on the right of expatriation, it required an Act of Congress in 1868 to settle the question by proclaiming expatriation "as a natural and inherent right of all people."

special verdict: A jury's conclusive finding of facts, which then left to the court the application of the law to the facts thus determined and the consequent entry of judgment. In *McIlvaine v. Coxe's Lessee*, the parties through their counsel agreed beforehand upon a written statement of the facts, which the Circuit Court jury, if actually empanelled, ratified without deliberating.

within a reasonable time: A traditional escape clause used by lawyers and judges to avoid the issue of determining how long is long enough—in the case of Daniel Coxe, how long remaining or "abiding" in New Jersey would result in his becoming a citizen of that state by implied consent.

writ of error: A means of taking an appeal to the Supreme Court of the United States from a decision of a lower federal court as prescribed in Section 22 of the Judiciary Act of 1789, requiring an authenticated transcript of the record, an assignment of errors, and a prayer for reversal, accompanied by a citation to the adverse party, signed by a judge of the court below or by a justice of the Supreme Court. Such was the route followed by Tench Coxe and his counsel in taking, as the **plaintiff in error,** the appeal to the Supreme Court, while Daniel Coxe's side, having prevailed at the Circuit Court level, became the **defendant in error** before the Supreme Court.

Index

www.ingramcontent.com/pod-product-compliance
Lightning Source LLC
Chambersburg PA
CBHW050349110426
42812CB00008B/2413